Contents

Part 1

Self-management

Chapter
Time management

Chapter ❷
Setting and achieving goals and objectives

Chapter ❸
Decision-making and problem-solving

Chapter 4
Creativity and innovation

Chapter 5
Part 1: Personal reminders and thoughts worth thinking

Part 2

Managing others

Chapter 6
Leadership and teambuilding

Chapter 7
Motivation and people management

Chapter ⑧
Communication and presentation

Chapter 9

Part 2: Personal reminders and thoughts worth thinking

Part 1

Self-management

Chapter

Chapter 1

Time management

Introduction

Time management is about managing your time with a focus on achievement: of doing and completing those things which you want to do and which need doing.

Time management is goal-driven and results oriented. Success in time management is measured by the quality of both your work and your personal life.

Tempus Fugit

Whilst it is true to say that life only makes sense in retrospect, it can be shaped by your sense of time and purpose. In keeping with business planning, *time* planning – and your approach to the use of your time (and to the extent that you can influence it, how others spend their time) – should be to avoid the trap of failing to plan, which is, in effect, planning to fail. In other words, if time is money, spend it wisely.

Basic approach to time management

You need to be certain that you:

- can define your business role and know what constitutes to a successful outcome
- spend time thinking and planning for yourself and others
- have a clear understanding of your business purpose
- know the balance you wish to achieve between your business and your private commitments (and can identify the time demands on both).

The Adair ten principles of time management

1 Develop a personal sense of time

2 Identify long-term goals

3 Make medium-term plans

4 Plan the day

5 Make the **best** use of your **best** time

6 Organise office work

7 Manage meetings

8 Delegate effectively

9 Make use of committed time

10 Manage your health

At all costs you should avoid falling into one of the following stereotypes:

- a poor delegator
- a bad organiser
- an excellent procrastinator
- a poor performer at meetings
- a purposeless executive.

Developing a personal sense of time

First audit how you spend your time, then analyse how you can improve your use of time.

Time audit

Keep a record (a daily time log) of where your time currently goes – break your day into fifteen minutes chunks for recording purposes. Do this for a week or so and review after each batch of three or four days.

Time Log	Date : *July 14*

	1 1300 *Lunch* ◯
8 0800	**2** 1400 *Called to MD's office – Spoke to Val re holiday* ◯ *Booking holiday by phone Working on next years budget*
9 0900 *Opened post* *Discussed club outing* *John* *Jan – Dictation*	**3** 1500 *Made telephone calls* ◯
10 1000 *Prepared for meeting*	**4** 1600 *Last minute letter for post. Read article in press. Talked to George re stock plan*
11 1100 *Meeting with client*	**5** 1700 *Call from client chasing order. Chasing above order. Started meeting report* ◯
12 1200 *Dealt with messages* *Went to lunch*	**6** 1800 *Went Home* ◯

Subject	Time Spent
Planned meetings inc preparation	*1½ hrs*
Unplanned / Informal meetings	*1½ hrs* ◯
Letters / messages / trouble shooting	*2¼ hrs*
Telephone	*1 hr*
Personal	*½ hr*
Writing	*½ hr*
Reading	*¼ hr*
Planning	*½ hr*
Lunch	*1¼ hr*

Reproduced from Keytime Time Management
with the kind permission of Keytime Management Developement

Peter Drucker's view is that only when we can manage time can we manage anything. In managing time we first need to know how we use it now and then change what and when we do things. Your time audit will probably confirm the findings of an IBM research which showed that the four activities that take up over 50% of the average executive's time are:

1   Meetings

2   Reading and writing business materials

3   Telephoning

4   Travelling.

Your time audit can identify these and others by using symbols ascribed to activities, for example:

M	Meetings (in committee form)
Mi	Meetings (in one-to-one interview form)
F	Finance and figure work
T	Telephone
Wr	Writing (reports)
Wd	Writing letters or dictation
T	Travelling
R&d	Research and development (including reading, training and thinking)
AOB	Any other business activity (should be specified)

Your time log can then be summarised in the following format:

Activity	Time Spent (in hours)	% of time	Comment (how to save time from now on)

Research indicates that we make assumptions about where our time goes and overestimate time spent on telephone calls, correspondence, report writing and planning, but underestimate time spent in meetings and one-to-one discussions. Keeping a record will confirm how you really spend your time and enable you to change how you spend it.

Analyse and improve your use of time

What elements can you readily identify which you can immediately change? Experience shows that improvements lie in changing the way you handle: interruptions (in person or by the telephone); meetings; travel; and incoming/outgoing mail. You can improve your use of time if you ensure that:

1   your time is spent according to a clear idea of your priorities and main responsibilities

2   you isolate the unimportant and ruthlessly prune out unnecessary or unproductive activities

3   you combine any 'free' time (ie free from meetings or other people's demands) to create meaningful and usable time of your own

4   tasks are simplified where others would not be adversely affected

5   you are not doing tasks which could be performed by others.

The balance of this chapter looks at how to ensure you improve your time management. The approach taken is to work from the long-term back to the immediate future, analysing your goals and gives time management tips on how to achieve them. (The approach works for both business and personal time management).

Identifying long-term goals

First of all, it is necessary to define your organisation's purpose and the purpose or your job, ie to what end is your time being expended.

Then, long-term goals can be set in terms of the results that the organisation wishes to achieve (and your role as part of those goals being achieved).

Defining the purpose of your organisation requires an answer to the basic question: why does this organisation exist? You should be able to write this business purpose down:

_____

_____

_____

Defining the purpose of your own jobs requires an answer to the question: why does my job exist? Again, you should be able to write this purpose down:

_____

_____

_____

Identifying long-term goals, the strategy of your business and your part in it, will result from pondering these questions:

Where   are we now?
do we want to be in 3 or 5 year's time?

What   strengths and weaknesses do we have?

How   can we improve?
can we get to where we want to be?

These same questions can be applied to your personal life

The answers to these questions will help you identify long-term goals. The longer the time frame the more fuzzy the goals become, so you should then reduce your field of vision to focus on tangible, attainable, definable and measurable goals, but not lose sight of the far ground.

You should reach a point where you can be clear about long-term aims/directions and medium, or short term goals/objectives which will be met and which will be part of a plan to continue on the road of achieving your longer-term aspirations.

Making medium–term plans

Your key areas of responsibility (and how your performance will be measured) should be listed and for each you must set objectives with time budgeted for each.

	Key area of responsibility	Objectives for each area of responsibility	Time budgeted to achieve each objective	Review of objective achievements
1	a b c	a b c	a b c	a b c
2	a b c	a b c	a b c	a b c
3	a b c	a b c	a b c	a b c
4	a b c	a b c	a b c	a b c
5	a b c	a b c	a b c	a b c

The review of objective achievement (the measure of your performance) should be at the intervals you have budgeted for each (eg 3, 6 or 12 months).

Smarter objectives

As a test of your objective-setting skills, remember they need to be **Smarter**, to the power of two, ie **Smarter**[2] :

Specific	**S**trategic
Measurable	**M**eaningful
Agreed	**A**ttainable
Realistic	**R**ewarding
Time-bounded	**T**eambuilding
Evaluated	**E**mpowering
Reviewed	**R**ewarding

Part of all this is to set out clear ways in which time management can be improved in the short to medium-term. A 'Time Norm' form can help here.

Task/activity/procedure	Time taken now	Target time

When measuring and assessing improvements you cannot lose sight of the cost and quality dimension. Time improvements should not compromise standards set for those elements. Real improvement comes from keeping all three at whatever is decided are the acceptable levels.

Being successful in making medium-term plans requires you to:

- know the context (the longer-term) in which you operate and how the medium and longer-term goals are linked
- be able to plan and implement activity
- set clear objectives and review progress toward them on a regular basis
- be flexible and adaptable to change in order to stay on course to meet objectives (unless you have changed those, too!)

Planning the day

The golden rule is to plan an outline for each day a week ahead, but plan for the day in detail the day/evening before it, or at the beginning of it.

In setting your programme for the day you need to establish **priorities** related to **urgency** and **importance**. If you then spend time according to how you have set your priorities, you will have addressed the important jobs – that is the art of time management.

The Adair urgency/importance matrix

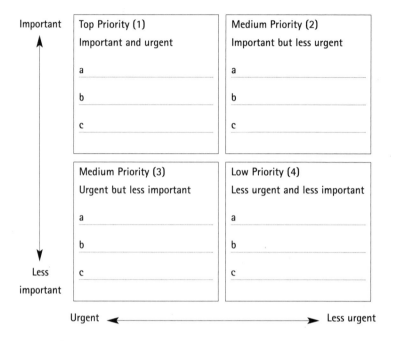

In the matrix you can identify tasks to:

1   do now

2   plan for (to use quality time)

3   do quickly (not requiring quality time)

4   do later or perhaps delegate.

This approach has also been called the Four-D system:

Drop it, Delay it, Delegate it or Do it.

You should shape your plan for the day by listing the various components, prioritising them and planning the time accordingly.

Your plan of action for the day should follow these rules:

- Make your plan at the end of the previous day or at the start of each day (whichever best suits you) enabling you to assess any unfinished work, together with upcoming priorities

- List the main elements (in relation to yesterday's, today's and the week's plans)

- Prioritise those main elements and identify tasks according to the matrix 1, 2, 3 and 4 above

- Group items together (eg telephone calls, correspondence)

- Decide when you will do the top priority tasks and block time out to do them

- Decide on remaining tasks (and share your plan with assistants/staff as relevant).

At a very basic level your list should also include your own system for identifying what **must** be done today, **should** be done today and what **might** be done today.

During the course of the day, regularly ask yourself whether you have changed priorities deliberately or whether you need to get back on course and tackle what remain as being prioritised activities.

Think of any daily list as a kind of shopping list – how are you going to feel going home without an item being ticked off as done?

However, do not be fixed and inflexible, provided you have managed your time and time has not mismanaged you.

Tips on daily planning

Tips on day-to-day planning and your programme centre on whether you are achieving at least your main priority activities.

If you are not, then consider:

- Are you unrealistic in trying to do too much?
- Were you unprepared (ie not ready) at the time you set to do the task?
- Was the task ill-defined?
- Did you find decision-making difficult (generally or for the task in question)?
- Were you lacking certain information?
- Is the neglect caused by too much time pressure?
- Did you 'give up' because of difficulty or boredom?

You should test whether your time budget made sense to start with, but if it did, then experience shows that the most common problem is interruptions. The most successful solution to interruptions is to learn to say 'No', remembering at the same time to be ruthless with time, but gracious with people.

Making the best use of your best time

You have certain times of the day when you perform consistently better than at other times. The Pareto Principle (which states that **significant** items of a given group form a relatively small part of the **total**) applies and 20% of your time produces 80% of your best quality output.

In making the best use of your best time, ie when you think straighter and are more alert, you need to know which part of your typical day it is that you can best perform certain types of task. Decide and plan activities accordingly.

You should be able to answer these questions. Are you:

- a morning, afternoon or evening person?
- aware that short term memory is better in the morning?

- using the morning for words and figure work, when most people perform such work better than at other times?
- aware that we reach peak alertness at noon, or that we are manually more dextrous in the afternoon?

Planning breaks into your day (for coffee, lunch, walking around the office/factory to meet people) will help you to work in concentrated bursts. Creativity as well as in-depth work can be improved by managing your best times to do, or think about, the appropriate task. Be selfish about when and how you spend time on planned activities. Do not be afraid to work at unusual times if you find that it suits you, does not inconvenience others and is more productive.

Organising office work

The two key consumers of time are interruptions and paperwork. To learn how to be the victor rather than victim of these two thieves of time, you should follow these guidelines:

Dealing with interruptions

- meet people in their office whenever you can (you control your leaving time)
- stand rather than sit for casual visitors (this controls length of stay)
- keep a focus on time (mention the time you have available, refer to your next meeting and have a visible and watched clock)
- stick to the point and avoid butterflying from main topic to unrelated ones
- be firm in a pleasant way.

Dealing with paperwork

- do you see only what you should?
- do you keep your desk clear of extraneous paperwork?

- do you handle each piece of paper only once? (this one idea is known to save up to one hour per day or 220 hours a year!)

- do you prioritise your paperwork (into action, information, reading, or for the wastebin?)

- do you limit the amount of paperwork you generate for others?

- can you pick out salient points quickly and know when to skip read or read in-depth?

Other elements to improve your time management in the office

1   Arrange your office or office space for ease of work, comfort and efficiency. Few people give this any thought at all.

2   Clear desk policy – concentration is helped by doing one thing at a time so your desk should only have on it, the specific job that you are tackling at the time

3   Write effectively, keeping it short and simple by thinking of the main point first and ordering your thoughts for logical expression.

4   Telephone – keep a log to see how time efficient you are now! Then get used to *planning* for each call you make (the salient points you want to make); *grouping* incoming and outgoing calls (usually for the end of the day when people are less verbose); and use a timer (eg an egg timer – to keep all calls to a maximum of four minutes). Do not be afraid to put a block on incoming calls to reduce interruptions.

5   If you have an assistant, use him or her to deal with or to redirect (helpfully) any mail or callers (whether in person or on the telephone), where he/she or someone else could better deal with them. Strive for excellence not perfection, through your assistant.

Managing meetings

A Time Lord's approach to meetings is to confront three main issues:

- is the meeting strictly necessary at all?
- how much time (particularly mine) is it worth?
- will it run to time?

You must always have a clear idea of how much a meeting costs (in people's time, including your own) and whether it is worth it in results. For example, typical costs might be:

Salary p.a.	Per hour cost	Per day cost
£100,000	£60	£420
£50,000	£30	£210
£25,000	£15	£105
£12,500	£7.50	£52.50

(These figures are only based on salary levels and exclude overheads, to say nothing of the opportunity costs of attending meetings rather than spending time on other productive tasks.)

What then are the hallmarks of the successful manager of meetings?

- Meetings are planned ahead (who should attend and with the agenda and any useful papers being circulated in advance)
- Times for each item and of the meeting itself are set in advance (and adhered to)
- Minutes are concise and action-oriented (with responsibilities allocated)
- There is clarity of outcomes(s) (shared by all)
- Meetings are reviewed constantly for effectiveness
- The focus is on the positive
- You are a successful umpire and referee.

Before holding any meeting, ask yourself these five questions:

1 *Why* **are we meeting?**

2 *What* **would be the result of not having the meeting, or** *what* **should result from having it?**

3 *Who* **should attend?**

4 *How* **long should it be and** *how* **should it be structured?**

5 *When* **is the best time to hold it?**

You cannot ban all meetings, so you must manage them to get the best results. To do this you need to identify the type of meeting:

The Adair five types of meeting

1 **Briefing meetings**
to impart and share information, to clarify points and incorporate ideas from others

2 **Advisory meetings**
to gather views and advice and to outline or share any ideas

3 **'Council' meetings**
to make and share responsibility for decisions, resolving differences on the way

4 **Committee meetings**
to 'vote' decisions and reach compromises/ accommodations of different views on matters of common concern

5 **Negotiating meetings**
to reach decisions by bargaining with other party(ies) who are acting in their own best interest

You should decide what each type of meeting you are to be involved with actually is and plan to run each type as time efficiently as possible depending on their purpose.

Being aware of the cost of meetings will focus the mind and planning will focus your actions. Minutes to record actions agreed and responsibilities should be in a form to give ease of follow-up and subsequent checking.

Delegating effectively

Delegation is entrusting a job to another who is also given the authority to do it. It is vital to be clear that delegation is not abdication – to give up your power to another would be an evasion of responsibility.

The benefits of delegation are that it gives you more time to carry out your key functions and to develop your subordinates. You are freed to spend more time on management and leadership and you are able to concentrate on such areas as:

- strategic and development issues

- knotty problems

- staff appointments/development/training

- key marketing/quality issues

- emerging from your office to hear what staff/customers can tell you about your business

- communicating with more of your staff.

Deciding what to delegate

You should select the type of work for delegation and consider to whom it can be delegated.

Type of work	Delegation to enact
1 Technical/specialist work	
a _____	a _____
b _____	b _____
c _____	c _____
2 Administrative/minor decisions	
a _____	a _____
b _____	b _____
c _____	c _____
3 Where others are more qualified	
a _____	a _____
b _____	b _____
c _____	c _____
4 Where staff development would result	
a _____	a _____
b _____	b _____
c _____	c _____

The seven main reasons why CEO's do not delegate were revealed by research in five European countries to be:

1   It is risky

2   We enjoy doing things

3   We dare not sit and think

4   It is a slow process

5   We like to be 'on top of everything'

6   Will our subordinates outstrip us?

7   'Nobody can do it as well as I can'.

So, what qualities must you have to be a good delegator?

There are five main tips:

1   **Choose the right staff**

2   **Train them**

3   **Take care in briefing them, and ensuring their understanding of the why and 'how to' of tasks delegated to them (and in imparting to them an understanding of business aims and policies)**

4   **Try not to interfere – stand back and support**

5   **Control in a sensible and sensitive manner by checking progress at agreed intervals.**

A checklist to test if you are an effective delegator

	YES	NO
Do you take work home evenings/weekends and/or work more than nine hours a day?		
Can you identify areas of work that you could/should delegate, but have not already done so?		
Do you define clearly the delegated tasks and satisfy yourself that the individual to whom they are delegated understands what is expected as an outcome?		
Can you trust people, or do you find it difficult to do so?		
Do you delegate authority and task?		
Do you think that the delegated task will not be done as well by anyone else?		
Do you involve those to whom tasks have been delegated in the whole planning and problem-solving process?		

Making use of committed time

You can increase your achievement level by using committed time (time that is 'booked' for example – travelling, meal-times) by: in the case of travelling time, ensuring that you use it to carry out, for example, reading, writing, thinking, meetings, making phone calls, listening to 'improvement' tapes; in the case of meal times, ensuring that you use them where relevant to hold business conversations or meetings.

In other words, you should establish productive activities to schedule alongside time which has to be committed to other activities, eg:

- Daily routines: use dressing, washing/shaving/meals etc by stimulating your mind eg with an improving tape

- Waiting time: do not waste it

- Travel time: use it productively

- Television: Do not let it consume too much of every evening.

Managing your health

Time management has to be as much about ensuring that you maximise the amount of time you have available to use as well as using the time wisely. That means taking steps to ensure you do not suffer time deprivation through illness of mind or body.

It is vital to look after your energy levels – regularly to top up your batteries – to discharge efficiently in a long-life fashion.

How topped-up are your batteries?

This is a five point test:

Sleep are you getting enough
(*Guide* – eight hours or slightly less with age)

Holidays – do you take and enjoy your full entitlement?

Eating habits – are you being sensible?
(*Guide* – moderation in all things)

Exercise – honestly what are you doing each week?
(*Guide* – three sessions of 20 minutes per week – even brisk walks – is a reasonable aim)

Thinking time – do you think about what you are doing in life and in work, even for a few minutes each day?

Stress

Time and stress are cyclists on the same tandem. Bad management of one pushes the other out of control.

You should **always** watch out for signs of stress in yourself and others... and take corrective action.

Warning bells should sound if any of the following are present in behavioural patterns:

1. Irritability
2. Ever-present anxiety/worry
3. Constant tiredness
4. Increased consumption:
   - alcohol
   - cigarettes
   - drugs
5. Over-eating or the loss of appetite
6. Memory lapses
7. Loss of a sense of humour
8. Feelings of nausea/fainting spells
9. Poor sleep patterns
10. Nail-biting, nervous mannerisms/'tics'
11. Feelings of tension and headaches
12. Indigestion
13. Loss of concentration
14. Unable to relax
15. Feeling unable to cope
16. Indecision
17. Erratic driving
18. Dependence on sleeping pills
19. Sweating for no apparent reason
20. Frequently crying or wanting to cry.

Research (in ten countries on a thousand managers) reveals that improving time management can help eliminate the 12 most common roots of stress in managers which are:

1. Time pressures and deadlines
2. Work overload
3. Inadequately trained subordinates
4. Long working hours
5. Attending meetings
6. Demands of work on private and social life
7. Keeping up with new technology
8. Holding beliefs conflicting with those of the organisation
9. Taking work home
10. Lack of power and influence
11. The amount of travel required by work
12. Doing a job below one's level of competence.

If you find yourself suffering from stress then you must:

1   **do something about it: look at the stress factors and assess what can be done to change your life at work/home.**

2   **express yourself: talk to people about how you are feeling and the concerns you have (even directly to a person who might be causing part of your stress).**

3   **evaluate priorities: check the balance of your life, take stock of activities and priorities and change them if necessary.**

4   **accept what you cannot control: have the courage to change the things that can be changed, the serenity to accept the things that cannot be changed and the wisdom to know the difference.**

5   **use your negative experience to positively change your behaviour.**

6   **use time management skills to take charge of your time and how it is spent, particularly making time to deal with stress causing problems. Get them out of the way.**

7   **count your blessings – list those things that you are pleased with, about yourself or achievements. Do not over concentrate on the past (guilt) or the future (anxiety).**

8   **ask yourself – what is the worst that can happen and can I cope with that? Use this to reduce anxiety about an issue.**

Summary and six-month follow-up test

Keep the Adair ten principles of time management in the forefront of your mind and in your planning and prioritising:

The Adair ten principles of time management

1	Develop a personal sense of time
2	Identify long-term goals
3	Make medium-term plans
4	Plan the day
5	Make the **best** use of your **best** time
6	Organise office work
7	Manage meetings
8	Delegate effectively
9	Make use of committed time
10	Manage your health

Six-month follow-up test

You should periodically test your time management skills by asking yourself these questions:

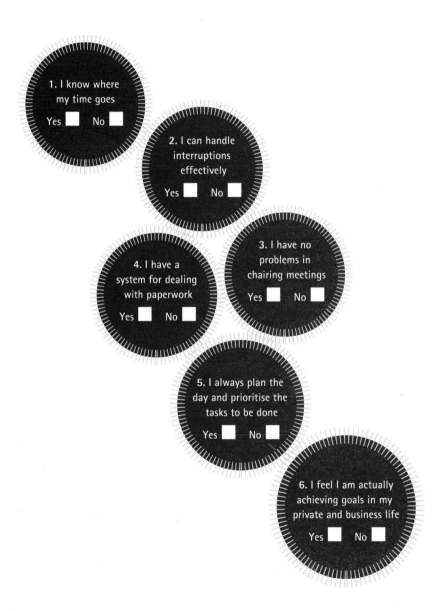

1. I know where my time goes
Yes ☐ No ☐

2. I can handle interruptions effectively
Yes ☐ No ☐

3. I have no problems in chairing meetings
Yes ☐ No ☐

4. I have a system for dealing with paperwork
Yes ☐ No ☐

5. I always plan the day and prioritise the tasks to be done
Yes ☐ No ☐

6. I feel I am actually achieving goals in my private and business life
Yes ☐ No ☐

Chapter 2

Setting and achieving goals and objectives

Introduction

In the chapter on Time management, the importance of identifying goals and making plans was outlined in relation to managing your time, in order to achieve the goals/objectives that you set and where the progress toward them could then be measured.

What do the words 'goal' and 'objective' mean? Defining them can assist in setting your goals/objectives.

A **goal** is the end towards which effort or ambition is directed. As a word it has its origins in 'the point marking the end of a race' or 'posts between which a ball is to be driven'. Goal-setting is a successful way to approach life-planning.

An **objective** (a word with military associations) is an end towards which effort is directed.

So goals/objectives define the end or purpose which is being aimed for.

Goals and objectives can be used in your personal *and* business/professional life and successful outcomes result from taking a strategic approach to your life and your work.

In a strategic approach, your aspirations need to be fixed in the form of goals/objectives. Strategy is then the way of devising plans and using stratagems (the devices/means) towards achieving the goals/objectives. (Objective and strategy are both words with military connotations and origins).

Personal goals and objectives

The starting point is to self-assess and take stock of yourself in the overall context of the direction you would like to be heading.

Personal Profile

1 *What are my strengths/what special skills do I have?*

_____

_____

_____

2 *What are my values (ie what is important and worthwhile to me)?*

_____

_____

_____

3 *What would be my preferred ways of earning a living?*

_____

_____

_____

4 *What activities/situations do I want to avoid?*

_____

_____

_____

5 *What achievements would I like to list as having been successfully met in my life?*

_____

_____

_____

6 *What would I like the highlights of my obituary to be? (This is a really good way of focusing the mind, as is asking yourself how you would like your epitaph to read).*

_____

_____

_____

Answering the above questions will enable you to set out more clearly the goals/objectives you want to achieve in your life and, linked with your time management skills, to plan the important steps to take to achieve them. You will then be able to 'add years to your life and more life to your years'.

Again the approach is to work from the long-term back to the short-term as in:

1 *What are my lifetime goals/objectives?*

_____

_____

_____

2 *What are my five-year goals/objectives?*

_____

_____

_____

3 *What goals/objectives will I set for achievement within one year?*

_____

_____

_____

Taking this approach will ensure that you concentrate on those goals/objectives which are important to you. The strategic element of your approach will then ensure that you analyse the obstacles that have to be overcome and plan your priorities and the ways/means to achieve your one year, five year and lifetime goals/objectives.

Answer these two 'questions' for each set of goals/objectives.

1 *Identify obstacles and opportunities:*

———————————————————————————————

———————————————————————————————

———————————————————————————————

2 *What are the ways/means to achieve goals/objectives, despite/because of those obstacles/opportunities?*

———————————————————————————————

———————————————————————————————

———————————————————————————————

This will give you your plan(s) of how to achieve your personal goals/objectives, which you must then implement!

Professional/business goals and objectives

You will find it helpful at this point to re-read the sections on **Identifying long-term goals** and **Making medium-term plans** in the section on Time management.

In setting and achieving professional/business goals and objectives you must:

- Define the purpose (of the business and of your role)
- Define your strategic aims

As has been seen, your strategic aims result from asking the questions:

Where	are we now?
	do we want to be in 3 or 5 year's time?
What	strengths and weaknesses do we have?
How	can we improve?
	can we get to where we want to be?

As for setting personal goals/objectives, your professional business goals/objectives (for your organisation and, perhaps separately, for yourself at work), should be delineated:

1 *What are the key long-term goals/objectives?*

_____

_____

_____

2 *What are the five year goals/objectives?*

_____

_____

_____

3 *What are the one year goals/objectives?*

_____

_____

_____

Then, plans/strategies have to be addressed as in:

1 *Identifying obstacles and opportunities:*

_____

_____

_____

2 *Analysing ways/means to achieve goals/objectives despite/because of those obstacles/opportunities:*

_____

_____

_____

Planning answers the question: 'How are we going to achieve' a particular task, meet a goal or reach an objective? How leads to who, what and when? You can then set out your:

3 Strategy for achieving –

a) short-term goals/objectives – the one year:

_____

_____

_____

b) medium-term goals/objectives – the five years:

_____

_____

_____

c) the long, long term goals/objectives:

_____

_____

_____

In the context of goals/objectives and strategy, there are a variety of different words/expressions used, as we have already demonstrated with the use of the words, **goals** and **objectives**. The ten key words in this area and what they suggest are:

1 *Goal*: the selected result to be achieved only with effort

2 *Objective*: tangible, attainable end toward which effort is expended

3 *Purpose*: the desired result or movement toward it

4 *Aim*: the target aimed at

5 *End*: the intended effects of actions (as opposed to means)

6 *Object*: the same as end, but also conveys wish and motive

7 **Mission**: the purpose for which the individual or organisation was 'sent'

8 **Plan**: set of ideas to achieve desired result

9 **Vision**: a concept denoting clarity of foresight/sharpness of understanding of a scheme

10 **Intention**: what is in mind to do.

In order to reach the goals/objectives set, you will need to identify them clearly. The hallmarks of good goals/objectives (see also the **SMARTER**[2] test in the earlier section on Making medium-term plans) are as follows:

Goals/objectives must be:
Clear, specific, measurable, attainable, written, time-bounded, realistic, challenging, agreed, consistent, worthwhile and participative.

Attaining goals/objectives brings into play strategy and planning, for which you need imagination, a sense of reality, power of analysis and what has been described as helicopter vision (the ability to see matters in detail, but from a higher perspective).

An operational plan/strategy should contain:

• a **SMARTER**[2] set of goals/objectives

• plans/stratagems for achieving them

The plan should detail all the steps required to complete those tasks which are needed to be done in order to meet the objectives set.

Time spent on planning is crucial in the thinking, the brainstorming and the sharing of ideas, the definition of purpose, the identification of obstacles and the ways and means of overcoming them and of meeting objectives.

It is necessary, of course, to get the right balance between **planning** and **implementation**. Planning saves time at the strategic and operational level and the key principle is 'every moment spent planning saves three or four in execution'.

Summary and six-month follow-up test

This chapter has sought to emphasise that in your business/professional and your personal life you must:

- set goals/objectives (short, medium and long-term)
- create plan(s) to achieve them
- implement the plan(s) and achieve them.

Six-month follow-up test

Chapter 3

Decision-making and problem-solving

Introduction

Decision-making, along with leadership and communication is one of the top three attributes a successful manager needs. It is a direct result of 'thinking' and you need to be able to 'think until it hurts'.

Decision-making is directed to reaching a goal/objective. It is about the how, what, why, when (and where) of a course of action and of how to overcome obstacles and to solve problems. Decision-making is what turns thought into action: it implies change and requires a decision to be made against a background of uncertainty and risk.

(In this chapter the use of the term 'decision-making' embraces 'problem-solving'.)

Decision-making skills

You need to be able to choose the action or course of action that is the best for you/your organisation to meet its objective(s). An effective decision is one that produces the goods, ie gives the desired end result.

It is important to be able to project ahead, to take the expected and unexpected into account, to have contingency plans in case events intrude in such a way as will turn a good decision into a bad one.

There are usually several different decisions that can be taken and pressure to decide. Decide you must, even if trial and error are then used to assess the decision, amend it or overturn it.

Fear of failure must not serve to make you risk-averse, rather it should push you harder to 'think until it hurts'.

The effective decision has these six elements:

1 **Defining the objective**

2 **Gathering sufficient information**

3 **Identifying the feasible options**

4   Evaluating those options

5   Making the decision (choosing an option)

6   Testing its implementation: by feel, by measurement and by assessment.

You should also listen to your 'feel-right?' test – do warning lights flash or alarm bells sound? If so, re-work decision elements 1-6. (Experience of your own or that of others helps to develop your 'feel' for decisions).

A decision is only effective if it is implemented (and that means getting the desired results through people). For that, other people need to be included in the decision-making process. You need to develop your skills in appreciating when it is most appropriate to include others in the decision-making process.

An effective decision-maker is always an effective thinker. The three essential skills are those of:

1   analysing

2   synthesising

3   valuing.

An effective decision-maker knows that quick decisions are not necessarily the best ones and decisiveness only results from thinking things through. Key decisions (and recognising when you are being asked to make or be involved in the making of key decisions) demand that great care must go into **analysing** (the component elements), **synthesising** (putting ideas together) and **valuing** (assessing relative worth).

The crucial elements in decision-making are:

•   establish the facts

•   consider the options

•   decide the course of action.

The truly effective thinker has these attributes:

1 **Skills of analysis, synthesis and valuing**

2 **Open to intuition**

3 **Imagination (to find new ways to overcome problems)**

4 **Creativity (coupled with careful preliminary work)**

5 **Open to new ideas**

6 **Humility – when to recognise that others may have better powers or knowledge and to combine with their thinking.**

To improve your performance you need to ask yourself how good your skills are (and have been) at:

- decision-making

- problem-solving

- creative thinking.

Do you make false assumptions and jump to conclusions or are you prone to faulty reasoning or to not listening to others?

Two maxims are useful in decision-making:

- 'It can be done'

- 'Always try to turn a disadvantage into an advantage.'

Always operate in the context of facing reality and of seeking and speaking the truth.

The Manager as decision-maker

Management can be said to be 'deciding what to do and getting it done'.

Success in business stems from good quality management decisions first of all and then the effectiveness in implementation which depends on the skills of leadership, influencing, communication and motivation.

One survey (of 200 leaders of industry and commerce) ranked 'the ability to take decisions' as the most important attribute of top management.

The logical or rational manager will invariably follow this decision-making model:

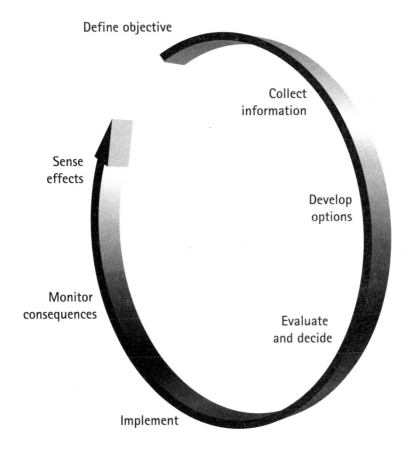

Define objective

Collect information

Sense effects

Develop options

Monitor consequences

Evaluate and decide

Implement

However, US research into decisions by public sector officials suggests that decision-makers rarely settle for the 'best' or optimum solution, being affected by emotion, power politics, the influences of other people and by their own values. Often a decision is a compromise between different courses of action, being one that:

- agrees to some extent with one's own personal interests, needs or values

- meets the value standards of superiors

- is acceptable to those affected (by the decision and for carrying it out)

- looks reasonable

- has an escape element of self-justification if it all goes wrong.

Clearly such approaches to decision-making must be removed from your approach!

Finally, managers need to be prepared to make time to think about decisions – to devote quality time to this crucial area of activity; to avoid superficiality (resulting from performing a great variety of tasks with little time to spare) because thought must be as important as action; and to involve other people (colleagues, subordinates and superiors) in making sensible management decisions.

Key elements of effective thinking and decision-making

Analysis

An essential ability in analysing is to be able to break the whole up into its component parts, particularly complex matters into its simple elements.

The hallmarks of the analytical mind are that it:

1 establishes the relationship between the parts and the whole

2 finds the root cause(s) of the problem

3 identifies the issue(s) at stake, the 'either/or' upon which a decision rests.

Analytical ability is improved by:

- working from first principles

- establishing the facts and separating them from opinions, assumptions or suppositions

- asking yourself questions (as in 'When did the problem first arise?' as well as our six friends Who, What, Why, When, Where and How?

- constantly checking the premise and/or logical steps which can undermine good reasoning

- thinking backwards from the desired outcome

- organising the facts

- seeing the problem as a solution in disguise.

Analysis is not, however, an end in itself and trying to over-analyse can lead to inactivity or 'paralysis by analysis' as it has been called.

Synthesis

Decision-making requires an individual to 'take a view' and that depends on the ability to combine parts or elements to form a whole: synthesis. Holistic is a useful word to use in this regard as it also conveys the approach, especially in business, which recognises that 'wholes' are produced by grouping various units together where it is difficult to analyse them into their parts without losing this wholeness. Hence an holistic view needs to be taken in business decision-making.

One difficulty is that analysis can be the enemy of synthesis (holism) and vice versa. There is a need in business to be able to see the wood for the trees (holism) rather than only the trees (analysis).

In this sense, and in business too, the whole is greater than the sum of its parts. Business thinking is a good example of the Gestalt approach whereby we arrive at an understanding of:

- the overall significance rather than a mechanistic explanation

- the relationships between events not just the events themselves which do not occur in isolation, only in a setting which gives each significance.

Managers need to take this whole view – not to see things as a marketing problem, or a production issue, or a stock control difficulty, or a people problem, or a management failure. Look at the whole to see what that can yield by way of a solutions.

Integration of facts, ideas and opinions is like the ability to synthesise and strengthens the manager's decision-making. Particularly in assessing financial performance, a manager needs to view the figures as a whole as well as in detail.

Other useful approaches

Imagination

This is an important attribute to have in business: the skill to visualise the whole in one's imagination. It is part and parcel of being creative in the approach to decision-making. Being imaginative is a crucial ability to develop in oneself and others: it helps to surprise the competition, to exploit the unexpected, to invent new products or services, or to solve problems creatively. Indicators of a healthy level of imagination are the abilities to:

- recall events easily and visually

- foresee what may happen before an event

- be inventive or creative artistically, mechanically or verbally

- fantasise about future events.

These elements of recall, visualising, creating, foreseeing and fantasising contribute to effective thinking in business as much as in the arts or scientific fields.

Conceptual thinking

Although a **concept** may appear to be an abstraction arrived at by analysis, it has a different feel because:

1 **it is a whole (and as such more than the sum of its parts); and**

2 **it is a developing entity in its own right.**

A concept is 'something conceived in the mind' and conceptual thinking in business addresses such issues as:

- What business are we in?

- What are its strengths/weaknesses?

- What are its purposes/aims?

Conceptual thinking should be kept separate from decision-making, even though decisions are made on the basis of the concepts that we have.

Concepts can be used in 'profiling' business development, but they then have to be made more specific in the form of proposals or plans, before being implemented. Concepts can be a way of taking your mind away from the particular and include the ideas of what ought to be as opposed to what is. Good quality concepts will underpin good quality business decisions. Therefore you should generate clear well-defined concepts and develop them.

Intuition

Being intuitive, successfully so, is undoubtedly a help in making effective decisions. It is not always possible to analyse problems into solutions and intuition is the useful power to know what has happened or what to do. Interestingly the powers of intuition are diminished by stress and general fatigue and so your ability to be insightful in decision-making can be adversely affected by these factors.

'Intuition', 'instinct', 'first impressions', 'feel', 'hunch' and 'flair' are important dimensions to explore when faced with not only decision-making, but also considering business activities and the systems to run them.

It is too easy to be dismissive of intuition, of being able to 'sense' what needs to be done or to 'smell' trouble/opportunities. Rather it is an invaluable key to making and taking effective decisions.

Originality and innovation

Creative and innovative thinking can help in making decisions that develop a business so they are elements to encourage in yourself and others. Be prepared to work at problems/issues to encourage creativity or insight coming into play and be prepared to encourage new ideas (by rewarding those who put them forward), to try out and innovate new products/services as well as new ways of doing things.

The concept of value in decision-making

With analysis and synthesis, valuing is the third essential in effective thinking and decision-making. The ability to make decisions has two main aspects:

1   **To establish the truth or true facts; and**

2   **To know what to do.**

Time must be taken on the first, otherwise integrity, or the value of truth, is lost in the process. Thinking first and then deciding what to do is the correct order in decision making. Getting at the truth should make knowing what to do easier.

In many respects, it is better to behave as if truth is an object, that it must be discovered. The truth and valuing what one discovers, should be seen as 'objective' with one's own views and conditioning recognised and relied on or discounted as needs be.

When you rely on others, as managers so often do, you may have to sift information from their 'valuations' (information plus judgement). This is another form of valuing – of knowing who and when to trust to give you truth, or truth backed by acceptable value judgements. Questioning is a valid part of establishing the credentials of the adviser and the credibility of the advice. Can you trust the person to tell the truth backed by sufficient expertise or insight? You will learn by experience to recognise the people who:

- tell you what they think you want to hear

- express a view thinking it might agree with your own

- are watching their backs

- try to hide things.

Be scrupulous in establishing the truth – ask questions until you are satisfied you have it right.

You are good at valuing if you can say that invariably you have good judgement and the converse is also true. Knowing the truth or reality can then be followed by deciding what to do.

Also, beware of inaccurate figures (even from accounts departments!), errors in facts, figures and assumptions and specious assurances – all must be tested for accuracy and 'truth'.

Decision-making and weighing up the options

It is invariably necessary to choose a particular course of action out of a range of possible 'options'. What is the best way of ensuring that your own selection process is a sound one? The basic point here is that you should never assume that there is only one option open to you. Consider a number of options (or as many sensible and pertinent ones as you can muster), many of which will be directly dictated or affected by the facts that you can establish. Gathering information also helps the collection of options, even considering options that you might think are closed to you (eg increasing price, scrapping low-profit items etc).

Selecting and working through a range of options means considering:

- Which are the possible ones?

- Which of those are feasible?

- How to reduce feasible options to two choices, the 'either/or'?

- Which one to choose (or a mixture)?

- Whether any action is really necessary at all, now, later?

- Whether or not to keep options open, ie not to choose yet?

You should avoid any compulsion to take action through an option where no action would be better and you should avoid assuming that there are only two possibilities, until you have weighed up all the feasible ones you can in a reasonable time-frame.

Whilst considering the options beware false assumptions: test all for validity.

At the same time, it is essential to understand the other factors which can limit the range and choice of options or their applicability. Judgement (again beware false assumptions – including about these factors) is needed about:

1 **Time**

2 **Information**

3 **Resources**

4 **Knowledge.**

You have to know the real (not assumed) limits which the above factors can impose on the options available to you.

Generating options, particularly if, initially, there seems to be only one, will usually lead to better decision-making. This is where imagination, creative-thinking and intuition can help.

Considering fresh possibilities and suspending judgement whilst generating them (through brainstorming) can increase the range of options by avoiding negativity as in:

- 'It won't work'
- 'We do it this way'
- 'It can't be done'
- 'It failed before'.

In weighing the options you must refine your skills at considering the consequences, both the possible and the probable. This will lead to assessment of risk and reward and both should be carefully calculated.

Can you accept the risk of failure – what is the worst that can happen if it fails and can I accept it?

Judgement then is used in selecting from the range of options which have been carefully weighed and assessed as to their probable outcomes.

It can be useful to clarify options or, in decision-making to seek to test by argument or discussion. If done in the right way clarity can be the result.

Disagreement should be encouraged, not for its own sake of course, but to stimulate ideas. Discussion prior to action should not be feared, but arguing badly (for example: being personal, over pernickety, seeking to procrastinate unnecessarily etc.) should be avoided.

Summary and six-month follow-up test

define objective

check information

implement

Do you have a
five point plan
approach to
decision-making
and problem-solving?

evaluate
and decide

develop options

Six-month follow up test

DO YOU USE

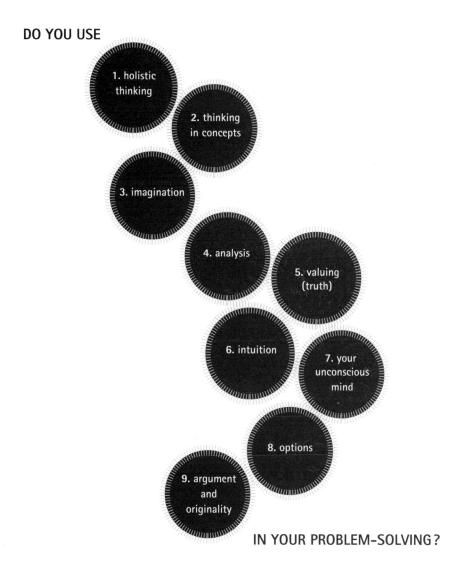

1. holistic thinking

2. thinking in concepts

3. imagination

4. analysis

5. valuing (truth)

6. intuition

7. your unconscious mind

8. options

9. argument and originality

IN YOUR PROBLEM-SOLVING?

Chapter 4

Creativity and innovation

Introduction

Really good managers (and all successful businesses have them) are capable of having, or recognising, good ideas and using them to make things happen in a new way: of translating ideas into useful, practicable and commercial products, services or systems.

Innovation (to bring in or introduce something new – a new idea, method or device) draws together new ideas *and* their implementation, whereas creativity is the having of new ideas which, in an organisation, are generated or spotted by individuals or teams.

It is important to:

- understand creativity and creative processes
- eliminate impediments to creativity
- widen the field of view
- build on ideas not merely criticise them
- tolerate doubts and uncertainties
- adopt a creative attitude in listening, observing and reading
- be confident in your own creative skills
- make time to think
- participate creatively as a leader, manager or member of a team
- use teams to innovate effectively
- manage innovation in your business.

This section of the book is divided into two parts: **creativity** (which looks at obstacles to creativity and ways to improve it personally and organisationally; and **innovation** (how best to manage creativity and innovate successfully in business).

Creativity

There are a number of *obstacles* which inhibit creativity. The seven main ones are:

1 **Negativity**

2 **Fear of failure**

3 **Lack of quality thinking time**

4 **Over-conformance with rules and regulations**

5 **Making assumptions**

6 **Applying too much logic**

7 **Thinking you are not creative.**

These obstacles can be seen in this identi-kit profile of the non-creative person; someone who is:

- not able to think positively about problems (and does not see them as opportunities)

- too busy or stressed to think objectively or at all

- very self-critical

- timid in putting forward a new idea (fearing ridicule)

- viewed as a conformist by friends/colleagues

- prone to apply logic as a first and last resort

- sceptical that many people are capable of being creative

- unable to think laterally

- uninspired even when confronted with a new idea.

On the other hand, creativity can be encouraged in people (including oneself) by exploring some of the qualities and characteristics of creative thinkers and the activities/steps that can be undertaken to improve the processes involved.

To be creative an individual should:

1   think beyond the invisible frameworks that surround problems /situations

2   recognise when assumptions are being made and challenge them

3   spot blinkered thinking and widen the field of vision (to draw on the experiences of other individuals/businesses)

4   develop/adapt ideas from more than one source

5   practice serendipity (finding valuable and agreeable things when not particularly seeking them) – having a wide attention span and range of interests is important

6   'transfer technology' from one field to another

7   be open/prepared to use chance or unpredictable things/events to advantage

8   explore thought processes and the key elements of the mind at work in analysing, valuing and synthesising

9   use his/her 'depth' mind (the unconscious mind) for example by sleeping on a problem to generate creative solutions to problems

10 note down thoughts/ideas that apparently drop into the mind unsolicited so that they are not forgotten

11 use analogy (to improve imaginative thinking) to find 'models' or solutions in 'nature', in existing products/services and/or in other organisations – not always reinventing the wheel

12 try, as appropriate, to sometimes make the strange familiar and the familiar strange to spark new ideas

13 make connections with points that are:
    •   apparently irrelevant
    •   disguised/buried or not easily accessible
    •   outside own sphere of expertise
    •   lacking authority

14 suspend judgement to encourage the creative process and avoid premature criticism – analysis and criticism repress creativity)

15 know when to leave a problem (remaining aware but detached) for solutions to emerge – patience is important here as is the suspension of judgement

16 tolerate ambiguity and occasionally live with doubt and uncertainty

17 stimulate own curiosity (in everything including travel) and the skills of observation, listening, reading and recording.

Managers should remember that creativity should challenge the status quo to test continuously for improvements, because:

- a thing is not right because we do it

- a method is not good because we use it

- equipment is not the best because we own it

Creativity can be improved by remembering that the creative process has four main stages and each needs to be properly 'worked':

1 **Preparation** (information gathering, analysis and solution exploration)

2 **Incubation** (letting the mind work to continue the process)

3 **Illumination** (inspiration – which can come when the individual is not necessarily thinking about the problem but is in a relaxed frame of mind)

4 **Verification** (testing ideas, solution, hunches, insights for applicability).

If ideas or solutions to problems are slow to come it sometimes can pay to leave matters alone for a while and reassess with:

- a new starting point;
- a different perspective;
- fresh motivation; and
- further consultation.

Innovation

It is worth identifying some of the key players who, if they were all present within an organisation would surely make it unbeatable.

Creative thinker: produces new and original ideas

Innovator: brings new products/services to the market or changes existing ones

Inventor: produces new and commercial ideas

Entrepreneur: conceives or receives ideas and translates them into business reality to exploit a market opportunity

Intrapreneur: responsible for innovation within an organisation

Champion: determination and commitment to implement an idea

Sponsor: backs an idea and helps remove obstacles

Successful businesses run on innovation and change and effective innovation requires:

1 **a blend of new ideas**

2 **the ability to get things done**

3 **sound commercial sense**

4   customer focus; and

5   a conducive organisational climate.

Managers should be able to:

- manage for creativity

- provide an organisational environment in which innovation can thrive

- use a variety of techniques to stimulate ideas for products / services/systems and to generate ideas for bringing them to fruition.

To manage innovation (and draw 'greatness' out of people, it must be seen as a process with three phases:

1   **The generation of ideas** (from individuals and teams)

2   **The harvesting of ideas** (people evaluating ideas)

3   **The implementation of ideas** (teams developing and introducing ideas to the final, customer-satisfied stage).

In innovation it must be remembered that creative thinking makes it possible and teamwork makes it happen. Successful innovation requires an organisation and its key managers to be able to perform five essential functions, these are as follows.

1   Recruit/select creative people

For the appropriate jobs, of course, you will need creative people and their characteristics tend to be:

- high general intelligence

- strongly motivated

- stimulated by challenge

- vocational in attitude to work

- able to hold contradictory ideas together in creative tension

- curious with good listening and observing skills
- able to think for themselves, independent in thought
- neither an introvert nor an extrovert, but rather in the middle
- interested in many areas/things.

Creative individuals thrive if they are:

1   appreciated and receive recognition

2   given freedom to work in their area(s) of greatest interest

3   allowed contact with stimulating colleagues

4   given stimulating projects to work on

5   free to make mistakes.

2 Encouragement of creativity in teams

It is not always easy to manage the creative and innovative aspects of teamwork, where individuals ideally need to share the values, characteristics and interests of the other team members, to work with them in harmony and yet have something different to offer.

Belbin identified nine team-member roles, some of which are relatively self-explanatory:

1   **Plant (solves difficult problems)**

2   **Resource Manager**

3   **Co-ordinator**

4   **Shaper**

5   **Monitor/Evaluator**

6   **Team Worker (co-operative, diplomatic)**

7   **Implementer**

8   **Completer**

9   **Specialist.**

A good team will exhibit all of the above 'roles', not necessarily with nine different people, but with fewer team members adopting different roles to complete the task.

Encouraging creativity in teams (besides helping individuals to 'perform' the Belbin roles within a team) depends on a manager's skills at:

- using the different skills within the team (having first identified the attributes of each individual)

- ensuring conflicts of ideas are allowed to happen and are tolerated by all

- recognising particularly good contributions

- helping the team generate ideas (eg by brainstorming)

- creating an open environment where individuals can speak up honestly.

3 Team training

Self-evidently important (to improve team performance) is the development of team creativity by improving an individual's skills in effective thinking, communication and in his/her own particular area of expertise/specialism.

4 Communicating about innovation

Feedback can maintain interest levels and information about progress made can stimulate further activity and more progress. Good communication can help improve creativity and innovation and should:

- stress importance of new ideas and show how business has improved because of their implementation

- indicate why ideas have been rejected/accepted

- give progress reports of ideas originated by individuals/teams

- recognise and reward appropriately for successful innovation.

5 Overcoming obstacles to innovation

Managers must ensure that creativity and innovation are not killed off by:

1   an initial response of outright condemnation, ridicule, rejection, damning criticism or faint praise

2   the vested interest of a particular person or department

3   too early an evaluation/judgement – sometimes suspending judgement early on can see an idea grow and reach a strong stage where it will work.

Managers who are creative and act in innovation-friendly ways have not only the usual leadership skills (of defining objectives, planning, controlling, supporting and reviewing in the areas of task, team and individual needs) but also are able to:

- accept risk

- work with half-formed ideas

- bend the rules

- respond quickly

- be enthusiastic (to motivate others).

Organisations and innovation

The business organisation itself has to provide an environment in which creativity and innovation can flourish and the five hallmarks of those organisations that actually are good at innovation (and not just paying lip service to it) are:

1   top level commitment

2   flexible in organisational structure

3   tolerant of failure (and not risk averse)

4   encouraging of team work and innovation

5   good at open and constructive communication.

'Managing innovation' is a 'challenge to management... especially top management and a touchstone of its competence' Peter Drucker

Organisations need to work at the main ingredients for success at managing innovation and apply themselves to the five hallmarks listed above.

1 Top level commitment

This must be visible and audible and top management must ensure that blocks are removed and that inhibiting bureaucracy/individuals does not foul up the process. Chief executives and senior managers must value new ideas and innovation and participate actively to ensure that all know of their commitment to positive and useful change. Sometimes the need for short-term profits can dull the edge of creativity and innovation. Only top management can prevent this happening – taking the long not the short-term view.

2 Flexible in organisational structure

The antithesis of the innovative organisation is the bureaucratic one and Weber's characteristics of bureaucratic organisations are as follows:

- authority is impersonal and formal
- strong emphasis on functional specialisation
- a rule for every eventuality
- strong emphasis on hierarchy and status

- clearly laid down procedures (red tape)

- proliferation of paperwork

- security of employment and advancement by seniority.

At the opposite end of the scale would be the flexible organisation which is one:

- capable of responding to changing situations

- where barriers between staff in different areas are minimized

- with a flat rather than pyramid organisational structure

- where decision making is pushed downwards to where the organisation meets its customers/suppliers

- with entrepreneurial flair present at all levels

- which can develop and test more than one solution to problems encountered

- with efficient rather than stifling monitoring systems

- which has enough 'discipline' to get things done

- which balances freedom and order.

3 Tolerant of failure

Innovation and risk go hand in hand. Management which goes into critical overdrive when mistakes occur (rather than analysing them to learn from the failures) smothers creativity and innovation. Risks can yield failure, but not taking risks can spell total disaster and an end to profits and growth.

Unless failure results from negligence, recklessness or complete incompetence, managers should not seek out scapegoats or exact revenge. Profits are the reward for taking risks and innovative organisations learn to live with risk.

4 Encouraging teamwork and innovation

In innovation it can be said that none of us is as good as all of us. Teamwork and innovation are better in organisations where:

- the climate is open

- participation is encouraged

- facts and information are readily available

- change is managed positively

- resources are provided for training and development

- rules are at a minimum (with policies and guidelines instead)

- internal communications are good and more by mouth than memo

- respect is given to all colleagues (but not on demand by management – it has to be earned)

- managers are themselves highly motivated

- teamwork often transcends departmental boundaries.

5 Good at open and constructive communication

Communication should be good laterally **and** vertically (and flatter organisations should – in theory, at least – encourage good lateral communication). Managers should ensure a good flow of information – ideas can emerge as a result. Cross-fertilisation can create more (and better) ideas, particularly where departmental, divisional boundaries are crossed.

Checklist for the innovative organisation

	YES	NO
Is the top management team committed to innovation?	☐	☐
Does the organisation express clearly its vision (which should include an emphasis on innovation)?	☐	☐
Is the Chief Executive openly enthusiastic for change?	☐	☐
Are mutual stimulation, feedback and constructive criticism all at high levels of activity?	☐	☐
Is the organisation good at team work including the use of project teams?	☐	☐
Are mistakes and failures accepted as part of risk-taking?	☐	☐
Do creative people join *and* stay with the organisation?	☐	☐
Is innovation rewarded (financially or by promotion or both)?	☐	☐
Are lateral communications good?	☐	☐
Can ideas be exchanged informally and are opportunities provided to do this?	☐	☐
Does the organisation raise excuses not to innovate?	☐	☐
Are resources given to new ideas?	☐	☐
Is the structure flexible?	☐	☐
Is decision-making pushed down to the lowest level at which decisions could be taken?	☐	☐
Do all staff see themselves as part of the creative and innovative processes?	☐	☐
Does the organisation take a long-term view of the benefits of innovation?	☐	☐
Is innovation part of the organisation's vision and strategy?	☐	☐
Is it fun to work in your organisation?	☐	☐

Scoring: Yes/No – More than 9 No scores – not good!

The Generation of ideas

It is interesting to note that organisations can get ideas from, amongst other sources:

- R&D (internal or external)
- Staff
- Competitors
- Suppliers
- Customers
- Quality circles.

One survey demonstrated that SMEs (small and medium sized enterprises) can get ideas from, in order of importance:

1 Staff

2 Customers

3 Market and competition

4 Board and Planning Group

5 Sales Department

6 Suppliers

7 Managing Director

8 Consultants

9 Shows and exhibitions.

Ideas have to be sieved – by individuals or by teams – to choose and refine the selected ideas to then develop them and take them to market.

Suggestion schemes can work provided people on all sides know that:

- all ideas from everyone will be listened to

- every idea deserves thanks

- some ideas will not work

- a forum for ideas assists the process of innovation.

Recognition (and selection) of ideas to be pursued should be on the basis that the idea can show:

- originality of thought

- ultimate benefit to the customer

- business potential

- quality improvement

- cost savings

- viability in implementation.

In sieving ideas, three questions should be asked (as Henry Ford did):

1 **Is it needed?**

2 **Is it practical?**

3 **Is it commercial?**

Project teams can drive an idea forward to its successful innovation by remembering three strategies which work and they are to:

1 **recruit a senior sponsor**

2 **run a pilot project or experiment**

3 **present innovation as a gradual/incremental development.**

Brainstorming (getting a large number of ideas from a group in a short time) can produce ideas (which then have to be sieved and tested) and Alexander Osborn's rules are hard to beat:

- Suspend judgement – no criticism or evaluation

- Free-wheel – anything goes, the wilder the better

- Quantity – the more ideas the merrier

- Combine and improve – link ideas, improve suggested ones.

In leading a brainstorming session the four main steps are:

1	**Introduce**	aim of session and remind people of Osborn's rules
2	**Warm-up**	if necessary do a practice exercise (eg 20 uses for a hammer)
3	**State the problem**	not too detailed
4	**Guide**	time to think
		generation of ideas
		no judgement/criticism/evaluation!
		clarify
		maintain free-flow of ideas

In leading a session which is 'sticky' and short of ideas to start with, ask 'what if' questions to stimulate thought.

Brainstorming sessions should always be followed up, perhaps in smaller groups and ideas should then be evaluated by:

- deciding the selection criteria

- selecting obvious winning ideas

- eliminating the unworkable ideas

- sifting ideas into groupings and selecting the best in each

- applying the selection criteria to obvious winners and 'best of' the various groups

- testing the selections by 'reverse brainstorming' (ie in how many ways can this idea fail?)

- informing the participants of further developments.

Successful brainstorming by managers can be achieved by asking yourself these questions:

1   **Do you use it whenever appropriate?**

2   **Does it work? If not, are you leading it effectively?**

3   **Is there a better person than you to lead a session?**

4   **Can you point to where brainstorming sessions have improved creative thinking in your organisation?**

5   **Do you and your managers have a list of problems that could benefit from brainstorming?**

6   **Do you use teams sufficiently to work on problems?**

In taking good ideas to market here are a number of questions you should apply to your organisation.

Checklist for the generation of ideas

	YES	NO
Is there an internal market for innovative ideas?	☐	☐
Do teams allocate time to consider ideas?	☐	☐
Do you and your teams spend time away from the office to review performance and plans?	☐	☐
Are customers/suppliers involved in innovation in your business?	☐	☐
Do you have successfully innovative teams and/or individuals and can you identify reasons for their success?	☐	☐
Do you have a suggestion scheme that works?	☐	☐
Are new ideas properly rewarded?	☐	☐
Do you help ensure ideas are not lost through poor presentation?	☐	☐
Do you know of an alternative route to profitability and growth other than through innovation?	☐	☐

Characteristics of innovators

As a manager you should possess these skills/qualities:

1 **A clear vision of required results**

2 **The ability to:**

- define objectives and benefits of ideas/projects
- present the case for it powerfully
- win support from superiors, colleagues and subordinates
- motivate people into action so that they contribute to project success
- influence others to support the project
- deal with criticism, interference, lack of enthusiasm, disputes and lateness

3 **Courage – to take risks (and endure any setbacks)**

4 **Willpower to maintain momentum**

5 **Fairness – to ensure all who participate are recognised/ rewarded.**

Summary and six-month follow-up test

The seven habits of successful creative thinkers are:

1   **Thinking outside the apparent confines of the problem/ situation**

2   **Welcoming chance intrusions**

3   **Listening to your depth mind (the unconscious mind)**

4   **Suspending judgement**

5   **Using the stepping stones of analogy**

6   **Tolerating ambiguity**

7   **Banking all ideas from all sources**

Innovation needs the generation, harvesting and implementation of ideas. Managers good at innovation accept risk, are flexible and are motivated to take ideas through to completion.

Six-month follow-up test

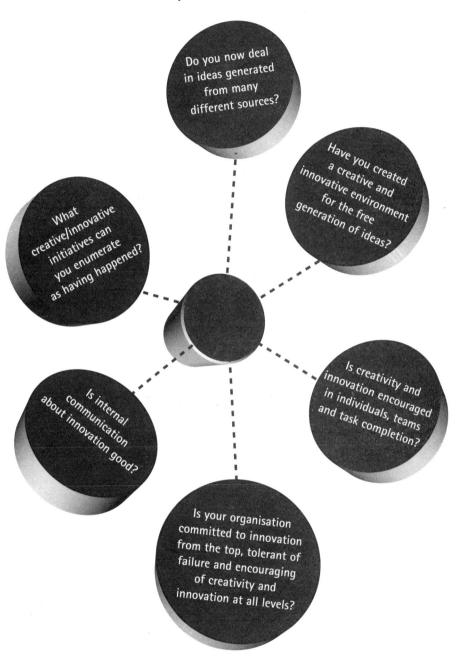

Do you now deal in ideas generated from many different sources?

Have you created a creative and innovative environment for the free generation of ideas?

What creative/innovative initiatives can you enumerate as having happened?

Is creativity and innovation encouraged in individuals, teams and task completion?

Is internal communication about innovation good?

Is your organisation committed to innovation from the top, tolerant of failure and encouraging of creativity and innovation at all levels?

Chapter 5

Part 1: Personal reminders and thoughts worth thinking

Introduction

This section will look at the main areas covered in the first part of the book and will offer:

i) personal reminders – points to bear in mind in pursuing your personal development, particularly to ensure that you achieve a balance between personal and business success; and

ii) thoughts worth thinking – quotes from various sources which shed light on the management topics covered in Part 1, which you might find helpful or inspiring.

Time management

i) Personal reminders

The Adair ten principles of time management		
Apply these principles to all parts of your life	1	Develop a personal sense of time
	2	Identify long-term goals
	3	Make medium-term plans
	4	Plan the day
	5	Make the **best** use of your **best** time
	6	Organise office work
	7	Manage meetings
	8	Delegate effectively
	9	Make use of committed time
	10	Manage your health

ii) Thoughts worth thinking

'Nothing really belongs to us but time,

which even he has who has nothing else'

Baltasar Gracian

'Time wasted is existence, used is life'

Edward Young

'I know what time is until someone asks me'

St Augustine

'Become time obsessed. Virtually all staff processes can be shortened by between 50 per cent and 99 per cent. Directly tie performance evaluations to speed. Remember: 'What gets measured gets done'. Make speed pay!' Tom Peters

> *'Never put off until tomorrow*
> *what you can do today.'*
>
> Lord Chesterfield

A personal sense of time

There is nothing which I wish more that you should know, and which fewer people do know, than the true use and value of time. It is in everybody's mouth, but in few people's practice. Every fool, who scatters away his whole time in nothing, utters, however, some trite commonplace sentence, of which there are millions, to prove, at once, the value and the fleetness of time. The sundials all over Europe have some ingenious inscriptions to that effect; so that nobody squanders away their time without hearing and seeing daily how necessary it is to employ well, and how irrecoverable it is if lost.

Lord Chesterfield • **Letters to His Son**

> *'Never leave till tomorrow*
> *which you can do today.'*
>
> Benjamin Franklin

'It's not enough to be busy.
The question is:
'What are you busy about?'

Henry Thoreau

'Time is the scarcest resource
and unless it is managed
nothing else can be managed.'

Peter Drucker

'If I were asked what one thing an executive could do that
would really, and quickly, make him more effective, make
him achieve more and make him enjoy what he's doing,
I'd say: 'Make sure you know where your time goes.
Don't depend on memory, it's treacherous.'

Peter Drucker

'An inch of **gold** cannot buy an **inch** of _time_'

Chinese proverb

He who every morning plans the transactions of the day and follows out that plan carries a thread that will guide him through the labyrinth of the most busy life. The orderly arrangement of his time is like a ray of light which darts itself through all his occupations. But where no plan is laid, where the disposal of time is surrendered merely to the chance of incidents, chaos will soon reign.

Victor Hugo

'It is not possible to hold the day. It is possible to lose it.'

Lines on a Sundial, 1695

'Do you love life? Then do not squander time, for that is the stuff life is made of.' Benjamin Franklin

'In the morning when I get up, the first thing I do is think to myself: what am I going to do today? So many things: I count them, think about them and to each I assign its time… I'd rather lose sleep than time, in the sense of the proper time for doing what has to be done… to watch the time, to devote oneself to business and never lose an hour of time… He who knows how not to waste time can do just about anything; and he who knows how to make use of time will be Lord of whatever he wants.'

Leon Alberti

'Doing the day's business in the day'

Wellington

'He slept beneath the moon,
He basked beneath the sun
He lived a life of going-to-do
And died with nothing done.'

Epitaph of James Albery (1838-1889)

'What wears one out
is not what one does
but what one doesn't do.'

Archbishop William Temple

'It is essential for the Cabinet to move on, leaving in its wake a trail of clear, crisp, uncompromising decisions. That is what government is about. And the challenge to democracy is to get it done quickly.'

Clement Attlee

'Time is a dressmaker specialising in alterations.'

Faith Baldwin

'Go, Sir, gallop, and don't forget that the world was made in six days. You can ask me for anything you like, except time.'

Napoleon

'Procrastination is the thief of time.'

English Proverb

'Time wastes our bodies and our wits,
But we waste Time, so we are quits.'

Lines on a Sundial, 1746

'Remember that time is **money!**'

Benjamin Franklin

Controlling the Cabinet

The Cabinet usually meets once a week. That should be enough for regular meetings, and should be if they grasp from the start what they are there for. They should be back at their work as soon as possible, and a Prime Minister should put as little as possible in their way. We started sharp at 11, and rose in time for lunch. Even in a crisis, another couple of meetings should be enough in the same week: if there is a crisis, the less talk the better.

The Prime Minister shouldn't speak too much himself in Cabinet. He should start the show or ask somebody else to do so, and then intervene only to bring out the more modest chaps who, despite their seniority, might say nothing if not asked. And the Prime Minister must sum up. Experienced Labour leaders should be pretty good at this; they have spent years attending debates at meetings of the Parliamentary Party and the National Executive, and have to sum those up. That takes some doing — good training for the Cabinet.

Particularly when a non-Cabinet Minster is asked to attend, especially if it is his first time, the Prime Minister may have to be cruel. The visitor may want to show how good he is, and go on too long. A good thing is to take no chance and ask him to send the Cabinet a paper in advance. The Prime Minister can then say, 'A very clear statement, Minister. Do you need to add anything?' in a firm tone of voice obviously expecting the answer, 'No'. If somebody else looks like making a speech, it is sound to nip in with 'Has anybody any objection?' If somebody starts to ramble, a quick, 'Are you objecting? You're not? Right. Next business,' and the Cabinet can move on.

Clement Attlee

'You cannot kill time without injuring eternity'

Henry Thoreau

'The unexpected caller, pleasant or unpleasant, disturbs the pattern of your time. That time is already allotted. Hence there is no time to help somebody who needs it, to relax and enjoy a chat on the street.

Enjoyment is always for *after* when all the jobs with deadlines, the letters to be answered, the calls to be made, have been despatched. But that time never comes. There are always more letters, deadlines, jobs and so life gets postponed until an indefinite after – until it is too late. A hamster on a treadmill has about the same sort of freedom.'

Dr Jonathon Steinberg

The daily miracle

Philosophers have explained space. They have not explained time. It is the inexplicable raw material of everything. With it, all is possible; without it, nothing. The supply of time is truly a daily miracle, an affair genuinely astonishing when one examines it. You wake up in the morning, and lo! your purse is magically filled with twenty-four hours of the unmanufactured tissue of the universe of your life! It is yours. It is the most precious of possessions. A highly singular commodity, showered upon you in a manner as singular as the commodity itself!

For remark! No one can take it from you. It is unstealable. And no one receives either more or less than you receive.

Talk about an ideal democracy! In the realm of time there is no aristocracy of wealth, and no aristocracy of intellect. Genius is never rewarded by even an extra hour a day. And there is no punishment. Waste your infinitely precious commodity as much as you will, and the supply will never be withheld from you. No mysterious power will say: 'This man is a fool, if not a knave. He does not deserve time; he shall be cut off at the meter'. It is more certain than government bonds, and payment of income is not affected by Sundays. Moreover, you cannot draw on the future. Impossible to get into debt! You can only waste the passing moment. You cannot waste tomorrow; it is kept for you. You cannot waste the next hour; it is kept for you.

I said the affair was a miracle. Is it not?

You have to live on this twenty-four hours of daily time. Out of it you have to spin health, pleasure, money, content, respect, and the evolution of your immortal soul. Its right use, its most effective use, is a matter of the highest urgency and of the most thrilling actuality. All depends on that.

Arnold Bennett

'Lord,

there's never enough time for everything.

Help

me to do a little less a little better.'

Anon

On turning over a new leaf

The most important preliminary to the task of arranging one's life so that one may live fully and comfortably within one's daily budget of twenty-four hours is the calm realisation of the extreme difficulty of the task, of the sacrifices and the endless effort which it demands. I cannot too strongly insist on this.

If you imagine that you will be able to achieve your ideal by ingeniously planning out a timetable with a pen on a piece of paper, you had better give up hope at once. If you are not prepared for discouragements and disillusions, if you will not be content with a small result for a big effort, then do not begin. Lie down again and resume the uneasy doze which you call your existence.

It is very sad, is it not, very depressing and sombre? And yet I think it is rather fine, too, this necessity for the tense bracing of the will before anything worth doing can be done. I rather like it myself. I feel it to be the chief thing that differentiates me from the cat by the fire.

'Well', you say, 'assume that I am braced for battle. Assume that I have carefully weighed and comprehended your ponderous remarks; how do I begin?' Dear sir, you simply begin. There is no magic method of beginning. If a man standing on the edge of a swimming-bath and wanting to jump into the cold water should ask you, 'How do I begin to jump?' you would merely reply, 'Just jump. Take hold of your nerves, and jump.'

As I have previously said, the chief beauty about the constant supply of time is that you cannot waste it in advance. The next year, the next day, the next hour are lying ready for you, as perfect, as unspoilt, as if you had never wasted or misapplied a single moment in all your career. Which fact is very gratifying and reassuring. You can turn over a new leaf every hour if you choose. Therefore no object is served in waiting till next week, or even until tomorrow. You may fancy that the water will be warmer next week. It won't. It will be colder.

Arnold Bennett

Setting and achieving goals and objectives

i) Personal reminders

1   Define the purpose

2   Define your strategic aims

3   Identify long-term goals

4   Make middle-term plans (for middle-term goal achievement on the road to long-term goal achievement)

5   Set goals and objectives

6   Know your values (and review them)

7   Budget your time

8   Review goals and objectives and progress in their achievement, regularly

9   Adjust plans and activities to achieve goals set/adjusted.

ii) Thoughts worth thinking

'If you do not know where you are going, you can take any road.'

Anon

'It is

wise

to look

ahead,

but foolish

to look

further than

you can

see.'

Winston Churchill

'If you want to make
anything happen you must
make time and space for it.'

Anon

a zest for living

If you want to enjoy one of the greatest luxuries in life, the luxury of having enough time, time to rest, time to think things through, time to get things done and know you have done them to the best of your ability, remember there is only one way. Take enough time to think and plan things in the order of their importance. Your life will take a new zest, you will add years to your life, and more life to your years. Let all your things have their places. Let each part of your business have its time.

Benjamin Franklin

Decision-making and problem-solving

i) Personal reminders

- The ability to take decisions – the most valuable skill in management
- The five point plan:
    - Define objective
    - Check information
    - Develop options
    - Evaluate and decide
    - Implement.
- Use: analysis, holistic thinking, thinking in concepts, imagination, valuing (truth), intuition, your unconscious mind, options, argument, originality
- Know your mind and develop your thinking skills.

ii) Thoughts worth thinking

'If I have any advice to pass on it is this: if one wants to be successful one must think until it hurts... Believe me, this is hard work and, from my close observation, I can say that there are few people indeed who are prepared to perform this arduous and tiring work.'

Roy Thomson

'When I go into any business deal my chief thoughts are on how I'm going to save myself if things go wrong.'

Paul Gretty

'The **final** act of **business** judgement is **intuitive.**'

Anon

'I take it we are all in complete agreement on the decision here ... then, I propose we postpone further discussion of this matter until our next meeting to give ourselves time to develop disagreement and perhaps gain some understanding of what the decision is about!'

Alfred P Sloan

'Rightly to be great is not to stir without great argument.'

Shakespeare

'Men sleep well in the Inn of Decision.'

Old Arab Proverb

Creativity and innovation

i) Personal reminders

The seven habits of successful creative thinkers are:

1 Thinking outside the apparent confines of the problem/situation

2 Welcoming chance intrusions

3 Listening to your depth mind (the unconscious mind)

4 Suspending judgement

5 Using the stepping stones of analogy

6 Tolerating ambiguity

7 Banking ideas from all sources

Innovation needs the generation, harvesting *and* implementation of ideas and managers good at innovation accept risk, are flexible and are motivated to take ideas through to completion.

iii) Thoughts worth thinking

'He that will not apply new remedies must accept new evils – for time is the greatest innovator.' Francis Bacon

'DARING IDEAS ARE LIKE CHESSMEN

moved forward.

THEY MAY BE BEATEN, BUT THEY MAY START A

winning game.' Goethe

'Experience has shown and a true philosophy will always show that a vast, perhaps the larger, portion of truth arises from the seemingly irrelevant.'

Edgar Allan Poe

'Discovery consists of seeing what everyone has seen and thinking what nobody has thought.'

Anon

'Thinking will always give you a reward, though not always what you expected.'

Roy Thomson

'In the case of the creative mind, it seems to me it is as if the intellect has withdrawn its guards from the gates. Ideas rush in pell mell and only then does it review and examine the multitude. You worthy critics, or whatever you may call yourselves, are ashamed or afraid of the momentary and passing madness found in all real creators... Hence your complaints of unfruitfulness – you reject too soon and discriminate too severely.'

Johann Schiller

'While the fisher sleeps, the net takes the fish.'

Old Greek Proverb

'A person would do well to carry a pencil in their pocket and write down the thoughts of the moment. Those that come unsought are commonly the most valuable and should be secured because they seldom return.'

Francis Bacon

'A new idea is delicate.
It can be killed by a sneer or a yawn:
it can be stabbed to death by a quip
and worried to death by a frown
on the right man's brow.' Charles Brower

'God

HIDES THINGS FROM US BY PUTTING THEM CLOSE TO US'

Old saying

'Criticism often takes from the tree caterpillars and blossoms together.'

Old saying

Don't be afraid of taking a big step – you cannot cross a chasm in two steps.'

David Lloyd-George

'The மnind

connects

things in

unbelievable

ways.'

George Benjamin

'A man without patience is a lamp without oil.'

Andres Segovia

'One should never impose one's views on a problem; one should rather study it and in time a solution will reveal itself.'

Albert Einstein

'I invented nothing: I rediscover.' Rodin

'As soon as a thought darts, I write it down.' Thomas Hobbes

'My chief job is to constantly stir or rekindle the curiosity of people that gets driven out by bureaucracy and formal schooling systems.' Akio Morito

'There is a great deal of unmapped country within us.'

English Proverb

'**Curiosity is one of the permanent and certain characteristics of a vigorous intellect.**' Samuel Johnson

'One doesn't discover new lands without consenting to lose sight of the shore for a very long time.' Andre Gide

'*I question.*'

Leonardo da Vinci's motto

'The disease of not listening.'

Shakespeare

'*Many ideas grow better when transplanted into another mind than in the one where they sprung up.*'

Oliver Wendell Holmes Jr

'Man never rises to great truths without enthusiasm.'

Vauvenargues

'The typical eye

sees the ten per cent bad

of an idea and overlooks

the ninety per cent good.'

Charles F Kettering

'More creativity is the only way to make
tomorrow better than today.'

Anon

The creative art thrives in an environment of mutual

stimulation, feedback and constructive criticism – in a

community of creativity.'

William T Brady

'Chance favours only the prepared mind.' Louis Pasteur

'Between the idea

And the reality...

Falls the Shadow.'

T S Eliot

'An established company which in an age demanding innovation is not capable of innovation is doomed to decline and extinction. And a management which in such a period does not know how to manage innovation is incompetent and unequal to its task. Managing innovation will increasingly become a challenge to management, and especially top management, and a touchstone of its competence.'

Peter Drucker

The most important of my discoveries have been suggested to me by failures.'

Sir Humphrey Davy

Innovation is a gamble!

Sydney Brenner

'Without real commitment from the top,

real innovation will be defeated again and again

by the policies, procedures and rituals

of almost any large organisation.'

Anon

There are costs and risks to a programme of action. But they are far less than the long-range risks and costs of comfortable inaction.' John F Kennedy

'The way to be safe is never to be secure.'

Benjamin Franklin

'Experience is the name we give our mistakes.'

Oscar Wilde

'What is honoured in a country will be cultivated there.'

Plato

'There is a natural opposition among men to anything they have not thought of themselves.'

Barnes Wallis

'People support what they help to create.'

Anon

'What's the secret of entrepreneurial success? It's knowing when to use OPB (Other People's Brains) and OPM (Other People's Money).'

J B Fugua

'Changing things is central to leadership. Changing them before anyone else is creativeness.'

Anon

'He that wrestles with us strengthens our nerves and sharpens our skill. Our antagonist is our helper.'

Edmund Burke

'He who dares **nothing,** for **need hope** **nothing.'**

English Proverb

Part 2

Managing others

Chapter

Chapter 6

Leadership and teambuilding

This chapter of the book is divided into two parts:

A. Leadership and **B. Teambuilding**.

A. Leadership

A survey of successful chief executives on the attributes most valuable at top levels of management indicated the following in order of rating:

1	*Ability to take decisions*	14	*Capacity to speak lucidly*
2	*LEADERSHIP*	15	*Astuteness*
3	*Integrity*	16	*Ability to administer efficiently*
4	*Enthusiasm*		
5	*Imagination*	17	*Open-mindedness*
6	*Willingness to work hard*	18	*Ability to 'stick to it'*
7	*Analytical ability*	19	*Willingness to work long hours*
8	*Understanding of others*		
9	*Ability to spot opportunities*	20	*Ambition*
10	*Ability to meet unpleasant situations*	21	*Single-mindedness*
		22	*Capacity for lucid writing*
11	*Ability to adapt quickly to change*	23	*Curiosity*
		24	*Skill with numbers*
12	*Willingness to take risks*	25	*Capacity for abstract thought*
13	*Enterprise*		

There is (has and probably always will be) a debate about the differences and overlaps of leadership and management. Current opinion is that they are different concepts but they overlap considerably.

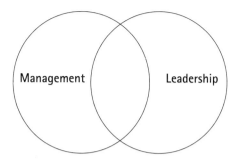

Perhaps management has the overtone of carrying out objectives laid down by someone else. It is certainly true that a well-managed business, in the sense of having perfect organisation, still needs that extra something.

Leadership has five distinctive nuances not found in management.

A leader must:

1 **Give direction**

2 **Provide inspiration**

3 **Build teams**

4 **Set an example**

5 **Be accepted.**

Henri Fayol (in 1916) divided the activities of an industrial company into six main groups:

1 **Technical:** production, manufacture, adaptation

2 **Commercial:** buying, selling, exchange

3 **Financial:** search for and optimum use of capital

4 **Security:** protection of property and people

5 **Accounting:** stocktaking, balance sheet, costs, statistics

6 **Administration:** forecasting and planning, organising, commanding, co-ordinating and controlling.

Good administration is the hallmark of good management and the proper and efficient use of resources. Managers become leaders when their personality and character, their knowledge and functional skills of leadership are recognised and accepted by the others involved.

Leadership can be 'specific to the particular situation' and its 'authority' can derive from:

1   **position (as in job title, rank or appointment),**

2   **personality (as in natural qualities of influence) and**

3   **knowledge (as in technical professional skills).**

Fayol listed these following qualities as being needed by a person in 'command'. A person in command should:

- have a thorough knowledge of employees
- eliminate the incompetent
- be well versed in the agreements binding the business and its employees
- set a good example
- conduct periodic audits of the organisation and use summarised charts to further this review
- bring together the chief assistants by means of conferences at which unity of direction and focusing of effort are provided for
- not become engrossed in detail
- aim at making unity, energy, initiative and loyalty prevail among all employees.

Qualities of leadership

A leader is the kind of person (with leadership qualities) who has the appropriate knowledge and skill to lead a group to achieve its ends willingly. This section looks at the qualities and functions of leadership.

Personality and character cannot be left out of leadership. There are certain generic leadership traits and seven important ones are:

Seven qualities of leadership

1   **Enthusiasm:**   try naming a leader without it!

2   **Integrity:**   meaning both personal wholeness and sticking to values outside yourself, primarily goodness and truth – this quality makes people trust a leader

3   **Toughness:**   demanding, with high standards, resilient, tenacious and with the aim of being respected (not necessarily popular)

4   **Fairness:**   impartial, rewarding / penalising performance without 'favourites', treating individuals differently but equally

5   **Warmth:**   the heart as well as the mind being engaged, loving what is being done *and* caring for people – cold fish do not make good leaders

6   **Humility:**   the opposite of arrogance, being a listener and without an overwhelming ego

7   **Confidence:**   not over-confidence (which leads to arrogance), but with self-confidence which people know whether you have or have not got it

In testing whether or not you have the basic qualities of leadership, you should ask yourself these questions.

	YES	NO
Do I possess the above mentioned seven qualities? (This 'test' will subsequently reveal whether or not you really do!)	☐	☐
Have I demonstrated that I am a responsible person?	☐	☐
Do I like the responsibility *and* the rewards of leadership?	☐	☐
Am I well-known for my enthusiasm at work?	☐	☐
Have I ever been described as having integrity?	☐	☐
Can I show that people think of me as a warm person?	☐	☐
Am I an active and socially participative person?	☐	☐
Do I have the self-confidence to take criticism, indifference and/or unpopularity from others?	☐	☐
Can I control my emotions and moods or do I let them control me?	☐	☐
Have I been dishonest or less than straight with people who work for me over the past six months?	☐	☐
Am I very introvert, very extrovert (or am I an ambivert – mixture of both – as leaders should be)?	☐	☐

If leadership depends on the situation, you need to ask yourself, whatever your qualities, whether you are right for the situation:

	YES	NO
Are your interests, aptitudes and temperament suited to your current field of work?	☐	☐
If not, can you identify one that would better suit you where you would emerge as a leader?	☐	☐
Do you have the 'authority of knowledge' in your current field (and have you acquired all the necessary professional and specialist skills through training that you could have done at this point in your career?)	☐	☐
Are you experienced in more than one field/industry/function?	☐	☐
Are you interested in fields adjacent and relevant to your own?	☐	☐
Do you read situations well and are you flexible in your approach to changes within your field?	☐	☐

Functions of leadership

In leadership, there are always three elements or variables:

1 **The leader:** qualities of personality and character

2 **The situation:** partly constant, partly varying

3 **The group:** the followers: their needs and values

This section of the book looks at leadership functions in relation to the needs of work groups. These needs can be seen as three overlapping needs:

1 **Task need:** to achieve the common task

2 **Team maintenance needs:** to be held together or to maintain themselves as a team

3 **Individual needs:** the needs which individuals bring with them into the group.

These three needs (the task, team and individual) are the watchwords of leadership and people expect their leaders to:

- help them achieve the common task

- build the synergy of teamwork and

- respond to individuals and meet their needs.

The **task** needs work groups or organisations to come into being because the task needs doing and cannot be done by one person alone. The task has needs because pressure is built up to accomplish it to avoid frustration in the people involved if they are prevented from completing it.

The **team maintenance** needs are present because the creation, promotion and retention of group/organisational cohesiveness is essential on the 'united we stand, divided we fall' principle.

The **individual** needs are the physical ones (salary) and the psychological ones of:

- recognition

- a sense of doing something worthwhile

- status

- the deeper need to give and to receive from other people in a working situation.

The Task, Team and Individual needs overlap:

This overlapping is evident in that:

- achieving the task – builds the team and satisfies the individuals
- if team maintenance fails (the team lacks cohesiveness) performance on the task is impaired and individual satisfaction is reduced
- if individual needs are not met – the team will lack cohesiveness and performance of the task will be impaired.

Leadership exists at different levels:

Team leadership:	of teams of about 5 to 20 people
Operational leadership:	a significant must in a business or organisation comprising a number of teams whose leaders report to you
Strategic leadership:	a whole business or organisation, with overall accountability for the levels of leadership below you.

At whatever level of leadership, Task, Team and Individual needs must be constantly thought about. To achieve the common task, maintain teamwork and satisfy the individuals, certain functions have to be performed. A function is what leaders *do* as opposed to a quality which is an aspect of what they *are*.

These functions (the functional approach to leadership, also called action-centred leadership) are:

- Defining the task
- Planning
- Briefing
- Controlling
- Evaluating
- Motivating
- Organising
- Providing an example

Leadership functions in relation to Task, Team and Individual can be represented by this diagram:

Leadership functions

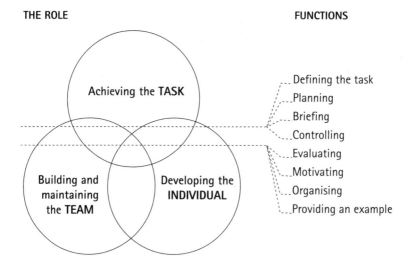

THE ROLE

FUNCTIONS

Achieving the TASK

Building and maintaining the TEAM

Developing the INDIVIDUAL

- Defining the task
- Planning
- Briefing
- Controlling
- Evaluating
- Motivating
- Organising
- Providing an example

These leadership functions need to be handled with excellence and this is achieved by performing those functions with increasing skill.

Before examining the skills of leadership, it is worth seeing where certain **qualities** of leadership can be viewed as having functional value. These can be examined as leadership characteristics.

Leadership characteristics

THE NEED	QUALITY	FUNCTIONAL VALUE
Task	Initiative	gets the group moving
	Perseverance	prevents the group giving up
	Efficiency	work done well knowing costs (energy, time and money)
	Honesty	establishing facts
	Self-confidence	facing facts
	Industry	steady application pays dividends
	Audacity	when not to be restrained by rules or convention
	Humility	facing up to mistakes and not blaming others
Team	Integrity	integrating the team and creating trust
	Humour	relieving tension and maintaining a sense of proportion
	Audacity	inspire through originality or verve
	Self-confidence	trusted by others
	Justice	fair dealing builds group discipline
	Honesty	wins respect
	Humility	not selfish, shares praise, not arrogant and divisive

Individual	Tact	sensitive in dealing with people
	Compassion	sympathetic awareness and help
	Consistency	people know where they stand
	Humility	recognises qualities/abilities and gives credit
	Honesty	wins individual respect
	Justice	fair-dealing encourages individuals

Leaders need to exhibit the following attributes/qualities/characteristics in exercising the functions:

1 **Group influence:** to generate a group willingness to achieve a desired goal/objective

2 **Command:** to decide upon a course of action as quickly as the situation demands and to carry it through with a firmness and strength of purpose

3 **Coolness:** to remain cool or unperturbed under testing or trying conditions

4 **Judgement:** ability to arrange available resources and information in a systematic and commonsense way to produce effective results

5 **Application/ responsibility:** to demonstrate sustained effort combined with a degree of dependability in order to complete a task or achieve an objective

Leadership skills

Having identified the main functions or principles of leadership, there are skills in providing those functions in different situations and managers need to develop their abilities to bring those skills to bear in increasing levels of excellence.

The eight functions (defining the task, planning, briefing, controlling, evaluating, motivating, organising and setting an example) will now be examined.

1 Defining the task

A task is something that needs to be done. People in organisations and teams need to have this distilled into an objective which is :

- clear
- concrete
- time-limited
- realistic
- challenging
- capable of evaluation.

There are five tests to apply to the defining of a task and they are:

i) Do you have a clear idea of the objectives of your group now and for the next few years/months which have been agreed with your boss?

ii) Do you understand the overall aims and purpose of the organisation?

iii) Can you set your group's objectives into the context of those larger intentions?

iv) Is your present main objective specific, defined in terms of time and as concrete/tangible as you can make it?

v) Will the team know for itself if it succeeds or fails and does it get speedy feedback of results?

In defining the task/communicating the objective you need to have the following abilities:

- To tell the group the objective you have been given
  BEWARE: *not understanding it yourself can lead to lack of clarity.*

- To tell the group what to do **and** why
  BEWARE: *giving the reason in terms of a past event rather than future.*

- To break down aims into objectives for other groups
  BEWARE: *not making them specific enough or not making sure there are enough objectives which add up to complete the aim.*

- To agree the objective
  BEWARE: *taking things for granted and not fixing on the objective.*

- To relate the aim to the purpose (to answer what and why questions)
  BEWARE: *confusing your division's aim with the purpose of the organisation.*

- To define the purpose and check that the aims relate to it and to each other
  BEWARE: *not doing it often enough.*

- To redefine the purpose to generalise it and create more aims and objectives
  BEWARE: *causing confusion by doing it too often or not knowing that it has to be done.*

- To communicate purpose to employees
  BEWARE: *using the wrong language, by-passing leaders below you or relying on others doing it for you.*

In defining the task, it needs to be broken down into objectives, aims and purpose so that it can be communicated with clarity. The end of the task should also be defined when the need arises and all should be aware of what the success criteria will be.

2 Planning

This key activity for any team or organisation requires a search for alternatives and that is best done with others in an open-minded, encouraging and creative way. Foreseeable contingencies should always be planned for.

Planning requires that the what, why, when, how, where and who questions are answered. Plans should be tested...

Checklist to test plans

	YES	NO
Have I called upon specialist advice?	☐	☐
Have all feasible courses of action been considered and weighed up in terms of resources needed/available and outcomes?	☐	☐
Has a programme been established which will achieve the objective?	☐	☐
Is there a provision for contingencies?	☐	☐
Were more creative solutions searched for as a basis for the plan?	☐	☐
Is the plan simple and as foolproof as possible, rather than complicated?	☐	☐
Does the plan include necessary preparation or training of the team and its members?	☐	☐

In ensuring that there is the appropriate level of participation in the planning process, the chart below may be useful:

The planning continuum

Use of authority by the leader

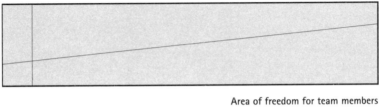

Area of freedom for team members

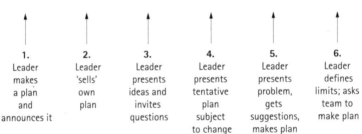

1.	2.	3.	4.	5.	6.
Leader makes a plan and announces it	Leader 'sells' own plan	Leader presents ideas and invites questions	Leader presents tentative plan subject to change	Leader presents problem, gets suggestions, makes plan	Leader defines limits; asks team to make plan

3 Briefing

Briefing or instructing a team is a basic leadership function conducted usually in a face-to-face way. Any briefing is an opportunity to:

- create the right **atmosphere**
- promote **teamwork**
- get to know, encourage and motivate each **individual**.

Before and after any briefing session, to ensure that the question of 'what is my role in all this?' (which will be on everyone's mind) is answered, you need to ask yourself these questions:

1   Does every individual know exactly what his/her job is?

2   Does each member of the team have clearly defined targets and performance standards agreed with me?

3   Does each person know at the end what is expected of him/her and how that contribution or that of his/her team fits in with the purposeful work of everyone else?

Communicating (speaking **and** listening) is crucial to get right in any briefing and it centres on the task, team and individual needs which should be addressed.

The effective speaking attributes of a successful briefing are to be:

• prepared

• clear

• simple

• vivid

• natural.

Assertiveness can be important. For example, to give the task direction and in explaining the role of the team/individual, especially in an initial briefing or where there is low morale.

In briefings, you could do worse than keep these points in mind:

The Adair short-course on leadership

1	The six most important words...	'I admit I made a mistake'.
2	The five most important words...	'I am proud of you'.
3	The four most important words ...	'What is your opinion?'
4	The three most important words...	'If you please'.
5	The two most important words...	'Thank you'.
6	The one most important word...	'We'.
7	The last, most *unimportant* word...	'I'.

4 Controlling

Excellent leaders get maximum results with the minimum of resources.

To control others, leaders need to exhibit self-control (but remembering that anger/sadness can be legitimate responses if the circumstances warrant it and are themselves mechanisms for control), to have good control systems (simple and effective to monitor financial and task performance) and to have control of what it is that others should and should not be doing in order to meet objectives. The success at directing, regulating, restraining or encouraging individual and team efforts on the task (and in meetings) are the criteria for testing a leader's effectiveness as a 'controller'.

A Checklist for testing controlling skills

	YES	NO
Do I maintain a balance between controlling too tightly or giving too much freedom to the team?	☐	☐
Am I able to co-ordinate work-in-progress, bringing together all the parts in proper relation with each other?	☐	☐
In technical work, do I ensure that team and individual needs are met?	☐	☐
Do meetings I chair run over time(s) allotted to topics?	☐	☐
Do I have proper budgets and ways of monitoring actual performance?	☐	☐
Do customers rate my organisation's control systems for:		
– quality of product/service	☐	☐
– delivery	☐	☐
– costs	☐	☐
– safety?	☐	☐

5 Evaluating

Leaders need to be good at:

- assessing the consequences
- evaluating team performance
- appraising and training individuals
- judging people.

In *assessing the consequences*, leaders should be able to foresee the outcome of action (or inaction) in terms of the technical, the financial and the human and to ask probing questions of the team in order to establish the likely consequences.

In *evaluating team performance*, perhaps through a de-briefing session after a particular project, the performance of the team as a whole in relation to the task can be examined:

- Has it been a success, a partial success or a failure?
- Can lessons be learnt?
- Can action be taken to improve performance?
- What feedback can be given to **ensure** improvement?

The evaluation of the team is helpful in trying to build it into a high-performance one where the hallmarks are:

- clear realistic objectives
- shared sense of purpose
- best use of resources
- atmosphere of openness
- handles failure
- rides out the storms.

In *appraising and training individuals*, the following agenda can be used:

- Past performance
- Future work to be done: targets, priorities, standards and strategies
- Matching perceptions of what can be expected by each party of the other in order to achieve a good working relationship
- Improving skill, knowledge, behaviour.

Some tips in handling appraisals:

- Have all necessary data available
- Put the other person at ease
- Control pace and direction of the interview
- Listen… listen… listen

- Avoid destructive criticism (encourage self-criticism)
- Review performance systematically
- Discuss future action
- Discuss potential/aspirations
- Identify training/development required
- Avoid common pitfalls, such as:
  - dominating the conversation
  - making promises unlikely to be kept
  - expecting dramatic changes overnight
  - blaming those not present.

In *judging people*, leaders decide who should do what and this always affects outcomes and so is a crucial skill. Leaders should not have favourites because:

- it destroys team unity
- the favourite is a personification of your judgement about people – if others do not agree with your judgement, your credibility suffers
- favourites advance by recognising the social and esteem needs of their bosses and by pandering to them – the boss can have his/her judgement impaired by this.

Judgement is improved by analysing impressions formed, discussing them with others and by making decisions about people more slowly and after deliberation.

In evaluation, you need to ensure that:

- your decision-making judgement is good
- you appraise people regularly and well
- you are good at judging people
- you evaluate your own performance as much as those who work for you.

6 Motivating

There are six key principles for motivating others:

1 **Be motivated yourself**

2 **Select people who are highly motivated**

3 **Set realistic and challenging targets**

4 **Remember that progress motivates**

5 **Provide fair rewards**

6 **Give recognition.**

Individuals are motivated by their requirements to satisfy a (Maslow's) hierarchy of needs:

- Physiological – hunger, thirst, sleep
- Safety – security, protection from danger
- Social – belonging, acceptance, social life, friendship and love
- Esteem – self-respect, achievement, status, recognition
- Self-actualisation – growth, accomplishment, personal development.

Each individual will be at a different stage/level up this hierarchy of needs and will need to be motivated accordingly.

Other than in financial terms, individuals are usually motivated if they can see that they will be given:

- achievement
- recognition
- job interest
- responsibility
- advancement.

A good leader provides the right climate and the opportunities for these needs to be met on an individual basis and this is perhaps the most difficult of a leader's challenges.

Leaders must also inspire others. In 1987, James Kouzes and Barry Posner identified five characteristics of what they call exemplary leaders:

1 **Leaders challenge the process. Leaders search for opportunities. They experiment and take risks, constantly challenging other people to exceed their own limitations.**

2 **Leaders inspire a shared vision. Leaders envision an enabling future and enlist people to join in that new direction.**

3 **Leaders enable others to act. Leaders strengthen others and foster collaboration.**

4 **Leaders model the way. Leaders set the example for people by their own leadership behaviour and they plan small wins to get the process moving.**

5 **Leaders encourage the heart. Leaders regard and recognize individual contributions and they celebrate team successes.**

7 Organising

Good leaders are good at:

- organising themselves – their own work and particularly how they manage themselves, their time and how they delegate

- organising the team – to build and maintain it to ensure that there is good, effective team-work

- organising the organisation – the structure and the systems/processes in which, and by which, people operate.

Leaders change things and organise for the achievement of results – leading change requires considerable powers and skills of leadership. In all aspects, leaders must organise with a purpose clearly in mind at all times.

Leaders should consider their organising skills by reference to the Task, Team and Individual as follows:

- **Task:**   **is there a common purpose?**
  - is it broken down into aims and objectives?
  - how is it/are they communicated?

- **Team:**   **what are the teams/sub-teams?**
  - how do they contribute to the purpose?
  - do they relate together as a team?

- **Individual:**   **do they have freedom and discretion?**
  - are individual needs being met?

Further questions in surveying your organisation are :

- Do the Task/Team/Individual circles overlap sufficiently to provide and maintain high morale in the face of difficulties?

- How are tensions resolved and are there adequate systems / disciplinary procedures/dispute handling methods in place?

The size of working teams/groups should be examined to assess the importance of these factors:

- Task/technology – complexity narrows the span of control, ie. is the team too big to control/handle this aspect and does it mesh properly with other teams?

- Communications – especially with geographical/physical dispersement, are they good enough?

- Motivation and autonomy – is the training commensurate with any wishes to be self-sufficient?

- Competence of leaders – are large teams led by good enough leaders, what are the leader's other commitments and does he/she have good/specialist support?

A Checklist to test the
organising function ability

YOU

Can you organise your personal and business life in ways
which would improve your effectiveness as a leader?

Do you delegate sufficiently?

Can you identify improvements in your time
management?

TEAM

Is the size and make-up correct?

Should a sub-team be set up?

Are opportunities/procedures in place to ensure
participation in decision-making?

Do you restructure and change individual's jobs as
appropriate?

ORGANISATION

Do you have a clear idea of its purpose and how the parts
should work together to achieve it?

Are effective systems in place for training/recruitment/
dismissal?

Do you carry out surveys into the size of teams, number
of leadership levels, growth of unnecessary complexity,
line and staff co-operation and properly working
communications systems?

Are you good at administration, recognising the
performance of administrators and ensuring that
administrative systems facilitate excellent performance
from teams/individuals?

8 Setting an example

'Leadership is example'. To be successful, a good leader must 'walk the talk'. Employees take a fraction of the time to know a leader as he/she takes to get to know them. The example you are giving is quite simply you. Whether this is a good or a bad example depends on the leader.

An example is set in verbal and non-verbal ways and all aspects of a leader's words and deeds must be considered in the light of this.

If example is contagious, it is worth ensuring that a good one is set to encourage the qualities sought in others.

Some key questions for good leadership are:

- **Task – do you lead from the front/by example?**
- **Team – do you develop your teams' standards through the power of example?**
- **Individual – do you view each individual as a leader in their own right?**

Bad example, particularly of hypocrisy, is noticed more than good, so care must be taken in all that a leader says and does.

A Checklist to test if
you set a good example

	YES	NO
Do you ask others to do what you would be unwilling to do yourself?	☐	☐
Do people comment on the good example you set in your work?	☐	☐
Does your (bad) example conflict with what all are trying to do?	☐	☐
Can you quote when you last deliberately set out to give a lead by example?	☐	☐
Can you think of ways you could lead by example?	☐	☐
Do you mention the importance of example to team leaders who report to you?	☐	☐

Developing leadership skills

Organisations (and if you are the leader of one that means you) should ensure that they have a policy of developing the leadership potential in all and particularly of newly appointed 'leaders'! Individuals should also ensure that they focus on developing their leadership skills by training, reading, analysing and following the example of good leaders and by assessing, monitoring and improving their own performance.

B. Teambuilding

This section looks at teambuilding from the leadership perspective and, as has been seen, teambuilding is part of the leadership 'holy' trinity of Task, Team and Individual.

One of the main results of good leadership is a good team:

Good leadership characteristics	Team outcomes
Enthusing	Team members are purposefully busy and have a basis to judge priorities
Lives values such as integrity	Gives a sense of excitement and achievement with people willing to take risks and higher work loads
Leads by example	Consistency in knowing leader's values
Generates good leaders from followers	Is trusted
Aware of own behaviour and environment	Aspire to leader's example
Intellect to meet job needs	Confidence in leadership
Aware of team and individual needs	The led start to lead (with leader less indispensable) being delegated to, coached and supported
Exhibits trust	Inspires confidence and performance
Represents the organisation to the team and vice versa	Confidence of contribution to aims and commitment to them

In 1985, ICI believed that the outcomes of effective leadership were that people will:

- have a clear sense of direction and work hard and effectively
- have confidence in their ability to achieve specific challenging objectives
- believe in and be identified with the organisation
- hold together when the going is rough
- have respect for and trust in managers
- adapt to the changing world

In achieving the task, building the team and developing the individual, whilst leadership **style** may differ, effective leadership (in ICI's findings and its development courses) emphasized that the leader must do the following:

- feel personally responsible for his/her human, financial and material resources
- be active in setting direction and accepting the risks of leadership
- be able to articulate direction and objectives clearly and keep his/her people in the picture
- use the appropriate behaviour and methods to gain commitment for the achievement of specific objectives
- maintain high standards of personal performance and demand high standards of performance from others.

Leaders in teambuilding provide the functions of:

- planning
- initiating
- controlling
- supporting
- informing
- evaluating.

In relation to teambuilding and the leader's role in terms of the Task, Team and Individual (which need to be addressed if the Team is to perform at high levels of achievement) the following three sets of questions will help analyse and improve the way that teams operate.

1 Task

Purpose:	Am I clear what the task is?
Responsibilities:	Am I clear what mine are?
Objectives:	Have I agreed these with my superior, the person accountable for the group?
Programme:	Have I worked one out to reach objectives?
Working conditions:	Are these right for the job?
Resources:	Are these adequate (authority, money, materials)?
Targets:	Has each member clearly defined and agreed them?

Authority:	Is the line of authority clear (Accountability chart)?
Training:	Are there any gaps in the specialist skills or abilities of individuals in the group required for the task?
Priorities:	Have I planned the time?
Progress:	Do I check this regularly and evaluate?
Supervision:	In case of my absence who covers for me?
Example:	Do I set standards by my behaviour?

2 Team

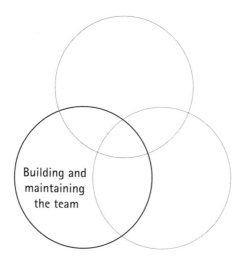

Objectives:	Does the team clearly understand and accept them?
Standards:	Do they know what standards of performance are expected?
Safety standards:	Do they know consequences of infringement?

Size of team:	Is the size correct?
Team members:	Are the right people working together? Is there a need for sub-groups to be constituted?
Team spirit:	Do I look for opportunities for building teamwork into jobs? Do methods of pay and bonus help to develop team spirit?
Discipline:	Are the rules seen to be reasonable? Am I fair and impartial in enforcing them?
Grievances:	Are grievances dealt with promptly? Do I take action on matters likely to disrupt the group?
Consultation:	Is this genuine? Do I encourage and welcome ideas and suggestions?
Briefing:	Is this regular? Does it cover current plans, progress and future developments?
Represent:	Am I prepared to represent the feelings of the group when required?
Support:	Do I visit people at their work when the team is apart? Do I then represent to the individual the whole team in my manner and encouragement?

3 Individual

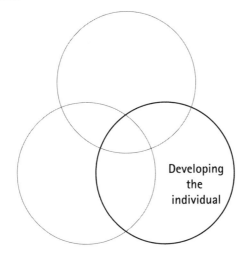

Developing
the
individual

Targets:	Have they been agreed and quantified?
Induction:	Does s/he really know the other team members and the organisation?
Achievement:	Does s/he know how his/her work contributes to the overall result?
Responsibilities:	Has s/he got a clear and accurate job description? Can I delegate more to him/her?
Authority:	Does s/he have sufficient authority for his/her task?
Training:	Has adequate provision been made for training or retraining both technical and as a team member?
Recognition:	Do I emphasise people's successes? In failure is criticism constructive?
Growth:	Does s/he see the chance of development? Does s/he see some pattern of career?

Performance:	Is this regularly reviewed?
Reward:	Are work, capacity and pay in balance?
The task:	Is s/he in the right job? Has s/he the necessary resources?
The person	Do I know this person well? What makes him/her different from others?
Time/attention	Do I spend enough with individuals listening, developing, counselling?
Grievances:	Are these dealt with promptly?
Security:	Does s/he know about pensions, redundancy and so on?
Appraisal:	Is the overall performance of each individual regularly reviewed in face-to-face discussion?

The good leader in teambuilding must act as:

- encourager
- harmoniser
- compromiser
- expediter/gatekeeper
- standard setter
- group observer/commentator
- follower.

As leader, there must be a clear understanding of:

i) **Team properties**

  - common background/history (or lack of it)
  - participation patterns
  - communication
  - cohesiveness
  - atmosphere
  - standards
  - structure
  - organisation
  - changes over time (forming, storming, norming and performing) both progressive and regressive
  - how to change the team properties in evidence.

ii) **Team roles being defined, but with room left for individual personality**

iii) **Team member functions**

  - distinction between content (the what) and process (the how) of group functioning
  - difference between behaviour related to the task and behaviour related to maintenance of the team and that behaviour which expresses individual idiosyncrasies
  - team leader functions (as above).

iv) **The individual**

  - balancing interests and self-expression of individuals and the team
  - the value of the task draws individuals/team together
  - having sound values motivates individuals in teams.

v) The overlapping needs of Task, Team and Individual need to be addressed

vi) Team processes

- to see what is really going on

- improved decision-making rests on seeing beneath the surface the pressures that influence the team

- calmness creates interdependence within the team and with the leader

- avoid team flight into abstractions

- aim for consensus (only where possible)

- assess team view of authority to see how processes/decisions are being affected by it.

vii) Teams within teams

- watch out for hostility, communication failure and mistrust as signs of team fragmentation

- develop teamwork between teams as well as within them

- winning can be as destructive to teams as losing, if not worse, unless both outcomes are handled well

- be aware of teams within teams and act accordingly to regain cohesiveness or sub-divide.

Summary and six-month follow up test

Summary

Leadership centres on:

- the leader – qualities of personality and character
- the situation – partly constant, partly varying
- the team – the followers: their needs and values
- the overlapping needs of the Task, Team and Individual
- leadership functions can be summarised as:
    - defining the task
    - planning
    - briefing
    - controlling
    - evaluating
    - motivating
    - organising
    - providing an example

Teambuilding centres on:

- achieving the task
- building and maintaining the team
- developing the individual.

Six-month follow-up test

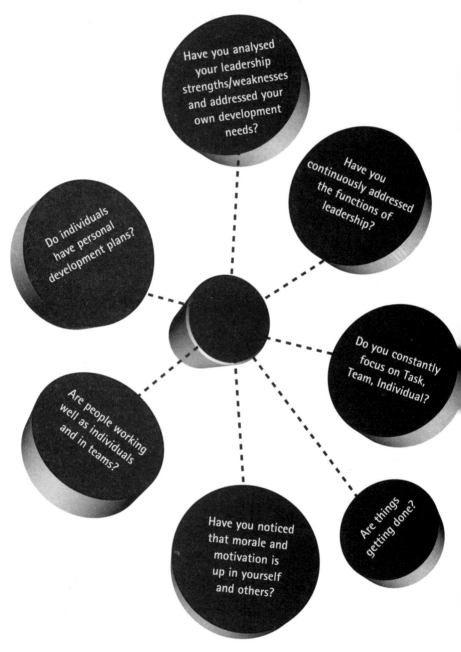

Have you analysed your leadership strengths/weaknesses and addressed your own development needs?

Have you continuously addressed the functions of leadership?

Do individuals have personal development plans?

Do you constantly focus on Task, Team, Individual?

Are people working well as individuals and in teams?

Have you noticed that morale and motivation is up in yourself and others?

Are things getting done?

Chapter 7

Motivation and people management

Introduction

Getting the best from people, achieving results through individuals and teams, maintaining consistent high performance, inspiring oneself and others into action – all depend on the skills of motivation. Self-motivation can be as difficult as motivating others and you cannot have one without the other.

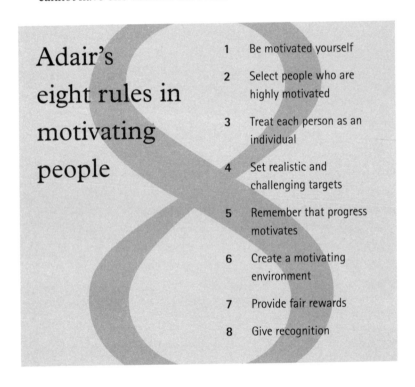

Adair's eight rules in motivating people

1 Be motivated yourself

2 Select people who are highly motivated

3 Treat each person as an individual

4 Set realistic and challenging targets

5 Remember that progress motivates

6 Create a motivating environment

7 Provide fair rewards

8 Give recognition

Understanding what moves an individual to action is crucial in a manager being able to engage the will to act. Motives (which operate the will which leads to action) are inner needs or desires and these can be conscious, semi-conscious or unconscious. Motives can be mixed, with several clustered around a primary motive.

The 50:50 rule

Just as the Pareto principle (or 80:20 rule) is the ratio of 'the vital few and trivial many', the Adair 50:50 rule has it that:

50% of motivation comes from within a person; and

50% from his or her environment, especially from the leadership encountered therein.

Unfortunately human behaviour and what decides/triggers it is more complicated than the carrot and stick 'theory' which deals only with external stimuli. The 'carrot' of reward/incentive and the 'stick' of fear of consequences reveal only two 'motives' which govern action. There are many more!

The expectancy theory – formulated by Edward C Tolman in the 1930s – (whereby behaviour rests on the instinctive tendency for individuals to balance the value of expected benefits against the expenditure of energy) falls into the same 'stimulous-response' approach to motivation. It does demonstrate, however, that an individual's strength of motivation can be affected by the expectations of outcomes from certain actions *and* further strengthened by the individuals preferred outcome, as demonstrated by Victor H. Vroom in the 1960s.

It pays, therefore, in external stimuli to bear in mind that:

1 **the routes to desired outcomes for individuals and teams are clear; and**

2 **individuals perceive the rewards or punishments in different ways according to their own values.**

This confirms the need to treat people as individuals but as the 50:50 rule also indicates, other motivational factors should always be set in the context of the individual's managed environment. Other theories of motivation which suggest that 90% of motivation is within an individual should be tempered by the 50:50 rule.

Needs and motivation

Maslow's hierarchy of needs

A sketch map of individual needs – which is useful for managers when considering individuals – can be drawn from Maslow's hierarchy of needs (1954), but it must be borne in mind that his theory does not fully appreciate individual differences or that each person has a unique set of needs and values.

Maslow identified five motivating factors in his hierarchy of needs and indicated that as each need is satisfied, others then emerge. He identified:

1   **physiological needs (including hunger, thirst, sleep)**

2   **safety needs (security and protection from danger)**

3   **social needs (belonging, acceptance, social life, friendship and love)**

4   **self-esteem (self-respect, achievement, status, recognition)**

5   **self-actualisation (growth, accomplishment, personal development).**

However, points to bear in mind are that:

- individuals do not necessarily move up the hierarchy on the principle that a 'satisfied need ceases to motivate' although that can be the case

- different levels of needs can kick in at random points on the scale toward full satisfaction of needs

- culture and age and other factors can affect the importance of the different needs to different people and at different stages in their lives

- the satisfying of some needs can be sacrificed in order to try and satisfy higher level needs.

McGregor's Theory X and Theory Y

In 1960 in his book 'The Human Side of Enterprise', McGregor demonstrated that the way in which managers manage depends on the assumptions made about human behaviour. He grouped these assumptions into Theory X and Theory Y.

Theory X – the traditional view of direction and control

i) The average human being has an inherent dislike of work and will avoid it if possible.

ii) Because of this dislike of work, most people must be coerced, controlled, directed, threatened with punishment to get them to give adequate effort toward the achievement of organisational objectives; and

iii) The average human being prefers to be directed, wishes to avoid responsibility, has relatively little ambition and wants security above all.

Theory Y – the integration of individual and organisational goals

(i) The expenditure of physical and mental effort in work is as natural as play or rest;

(ii) External control and the threat of punishment are not the only means for bringing about effort toward organisational objectives. People will exercise self-direction and self-control in the service of objectives to which they are committed;

(iii) Commitment to objectives is a function of the rewards associated with their achievement;

(iv) The average human being learns, under proper conditions, not only to accept, but to seek responsibility;

(v) The capacity to exercise a relatively high degree of imagination, ingenuity and creativity in the solution of organisational problems is widely, not narrowly, distributed in the population.

(vi) Under the conditions of modern industrial life, the intellectual potentialities of the average human being are only partially utilized.

McGregor drew on Maslow for much of Theory Y and put forward the cluster of features as an unproven hypothesis and further research was needed (Herzberg) to seek to prove it correct.

In terms of management in practice Theory Y does reveal that in any individual within an organisation there are untapped resources of goodwill, energy, creativity and intelligence.

Herzberg's Motivation – hygiene theory

In Herzberg's research (published in his 1959 book 'The Motivation to Work'), fourteen factors were identified to be the sources of good or bad feelings:

1 **Recognition**

2 **Achievement**

3 **Possibility of growth**

4 **Advancement**

5 **Salary**

6 **Interpersonal relations**

7 **Supervision – technical**

8 **Responsibility**

9 **Company policy and administration**

10 **Working conditions**

11 **Work itself**

12 **Factors in personal life**

13 **Status**

14 **Job security**

The eight **'hygiene'** factors, according to Herzberg, which can create job dissatisfaction are:

1 **Company policy and administration**
   - availability of clearly defined policies, especially those relating to people
   - adequacy of organisation and management

2 **Supervision – technical**
   - accessibility, competence and fairness of your superior

3 **Interpersonal relations**
   - relations with supervisors, subordinates and colleagues
   - quality of social life at work

4 **Salary**
   - total compensation package, such as wages, salary, pension, company car and other financially related benefits

5 **Status**
   - a person's position or rank in relation to others, symbolised by title, size of office or other tangible elements

6 **Job security**
   - freedom from insecurity, such as loss of position or loss of employment altogether

7 **Personal life**
   - the effect of a person's work on family life, eg stress, unsocial hours or moving house

8 **Working conditions**
   - the physical conditions in which you work
   - the amount of work
   - facilities available
   - environmental aspects eg ventilation, light, space, tools, noise

The six **motivating** factors that lead to job satisfaction were identified by Herzberg as being:

1 **Achievement**
   - specific successes, such as the successful completion of a job, solutions to problems, vindication and seeing the results of your work

2 **Recognition**
   - any act of recognition, whether notice or praise (separating recognition and reward from recognition with no reward)

3 **Possibility of growth**
   - changes in job where professional growth potential is increased

4 **Advancement**
   - changes which enhance position or status at work

5 **Responsibility**
   - being given real responsibility, matched with necessary authority to discharge it

6 **The work itself**
   - the actual doing of the job or phases of it.

The **hygiene** factors are those where people seek to avoid particular situations, whereas the **motivating** factors are matched with people's needs to achieve self-actualisation or self-realisation.

Satisfaction of the Herzberg motivators and avoidance of problems with the hygiene factors can help you as a manager to assess roles and jobs within your organisations to check what job-enrichment or empowerment you ought to contemplate to improve performance and give individuals greater job satisfaction.

Managers/leaders and motivation

Managers and leaders should take a realistic and visionary view of people who work for them and with them. Individuals can be managed better if it is recognised that they are:

1   individuals, but become fully developed and truly themselves in relation to other people and meaningful work

2   creative and imaginative, but only in concert with others through working on their own or in teams

3   driven by achievement (as individuals) but know that they achieve more as part of a team

4   self-motivated and self-directed but need management/ leadership (if only to co-ordinate activities)

5   intelligent enough to know the difference between rewards such as money and those less tangible rewards that meet value needs

6   interested in leaving work/the world a better place and know that that yields a bonus

As has been described in the relevant section earlier in the book, in leadership, the achievement of the task, the building and maintaining of the team and the development of the individual can only result from motivating people by providing the leadership functions of:

*   planning
*   initiating
*   controlling
*   supporting
*   informing
*   evaluating

and by being able to inspire others.

Managers should check that individuals have:

1   a sense of achievement in their job and feel that they are making a worthwhile contribution to the objective of the team

2   jobs which are challenging and demanding with responsibilities to match capabilities

3   adequate recognition for achievements

4   control over delegated duties

5   a feeling that they are developing along with growing experience and ability.

Manager's motivating checklist

DO YOU

YES   NO

Agree with subordinates their main targets and responsibilities together with standards of performance, so that you can both recognise achievement?

Recognise the contribution of each member of the team and encourage team members to do the same?

Acknowledge success and build on it?

Analyse set-backs, identifying what went well and giving constructive guidance to improve future performance?

Delegate as much as possible giving more discretion over decisions and accountability to a sub-group or individual?

Show those that work with you that you trust them or do you surround them with unnecessary controls?

Provide adequate opportunities for training and re-training if necessary?

Encourage each individual to develop his/her capacities to the full?

Getting the best from people

Be motivated yourself

Enthusiasm and motivation inspires others and the badges of good
example setting are that you should be :

- public – make sure you act in the open

- spontaneous – do not appear calculated

- expressive – do things because they are natural to you not for
  effect

- self-effacing – setting a good example is not glory-seeking.

Motivation is contagious so you should be infectious! If you are not
motivated yourself, you cannot motivate others and you should
examine the reasons why you lack motivation. Symptoms include
having little or no interest in the job, wanting to arrive late and leave
early, wanting to leave the job, feeling active dislike for it and feeling
out of place in it.

You can strengthen your motivation by reminding yourself:

1 to feel and act enthusiastically and in a committed way in your work

2 to take responsibility when things go wrong rather than blaming others

3 to identify ways you can lead by example

4 act on the 50:50 principle

5 to motivate by word and example rather than manipulation

6 set an example naturally rather than in a calculated way

7 not to give up easily

8 to ensure you are in the right job for your own abilities, interests and temperament

9 to be able to cite experiences where what you have said or done has had an inspirational effect on individuals, the team or the organisation

10 that the three badges of leadership are enthusiasm, commitment and perseverance.

Select people who are highly motivated

The seven key indicators of high motivation are:

1 energy – not necessarily extrovert but alertness and quiet resolve

2 commitment – to the common purpose

3 staying power – in the face of problems/difficulties/set-backs

4 skill – possession of skills indicates aims and ambitions

5 single-mindedness – energy applied in a single direction

6 enjoyment – goes hand in hand with motivation

7 responsibility – willingness to seek and accept it.

Choosing people well (and mistakes are made which should be confronted and remedied early) means looking at motivation, ability and personality and you should, when interviewing, look for real evidence behind the interviewee's facade.

Looking for the Michelangelo motive (where the quality of the work itself is a key motivator) can yield good results in selecting highly motivated individuals. You should look for:

- a sense of pride in the individual's own work

- an attention to detail

- a willingness to 'walk the extra mile' to get things right

- a total lack of the 'its good enough, let it go' mentality

- an inner direction or responsibility for the work (without the need for supervision)

- an ability to assess and evaluate own work, independently from the opinions of others.

It should be stressed that perfectionism is not what is called for – the best can be the enemy of the good.

Managers should check whether individuals are in the right job with the right skills and abilities, otherwise motivation techniques will fail. The aim is to select people who are motivated for the most appropriate job.

Treat each person as an individual

Find out what motivates an individual, do not rely on generalised theories or assumptions. Enter into a dialogue with each team member – help them to clarify what it is that motivates them – and use what you find to mutual benefit.

In each person you should engender a sense of:

- trust

- autonomy

- initiative
- industry
- integrity
- security.

Take time with each individual to:

- encourage
- hearten
- inspire
- support
- embolden
- stimulate.

Ask yourself these questions to ensure that you treat each person as an individual:

1   **Do you know the names of people on your team and their teams if they are leaders?**

2   **Can you identify ways in which those who report to you differ from each other?**

3   **Do you accept that an individual's motivation changes from time to time?**

4   **Do you spend time with people to know them, work with them, coach them?**

5   **Does your organisation see you as an individual?**

Set realistic and challenging targets

This can only be done in the context of understanding the organisation's aims or purpose. It is only then that targets and objectives can be identified and tasks defined.

Jacob's ladder model

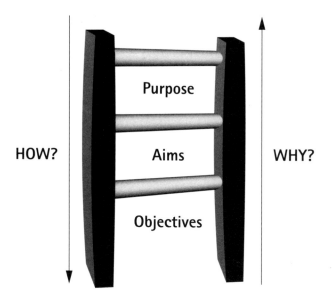

Moving **down** the ladder, ask **how** are we going to achieve the task? The answer is by breaking down the purpose into the main aims and the main aims into short and long-term objectives or goals.

Moving **up** the ladder, ask **why** are we doing this? The answer is to achieve this objective in order to achieve this aim and to satisfy this purpose.

Targets (for short and longer-term objectives) set should be:

- specific
- clear
- time-bounded.

An objective or target must be realistic (feasible) and challenging. If you aim for the best you can often get it.

Targets must be agreed and monitored with further action agreed to maintain motivation toward shared objectives.

Remember that progress motivates

There is a 'lust to finish' (John Wesley) and the key principle is that progress motivates – moving forward leads them to raise their game.

Feedback on progress (or even the relative lack of it) helps motivation either to spur people on or to concentrate the mind on what yet needs to be done.

Feedback is not given at all or sometimes not often enough, usually for these reasons:

- 'People don't need to be told how they are doing, they already know'
- 'People take it easy if you say things are going well'
- 'They are unhappy and cause trouble if you say things are not going well'
- 'We lack the skills or the time to do it'.

Feedback which is affirmative (praise) must be:

- accurate
- sincere
- generous
- spontaneous
- fair.

It must not be:

- patronising
- superior/condescending
- grudging
- calculated for effect.

Maintaining motivation depends on informing and inspiring and the rule is always to give information first, before you attempt to encourage.

Maintaining high morale is key to high motivation and morale covers the individuals and the team. Where an individual has low morale, the issues have to be addressed on an individual basis, but where group or team morale is low, the answer lies in deciding whether there is a lack of confidence:

- of ultimate success

- in the present plan(s)

- in the leadership/management

- in the minds of team members.

It can be necessary to remotivate the team by rebuilding self-confidence and by readdressing:

- aims – and clarifying objectives

- plans, resources needed

- leadership

- overlooked factors

- re-establishing the worth or value of the task(s)

- involvement of individuals in key decisions.

Create a motivating environment

Guidelines here are:

1 Beware of creating a restrictive organisation with an over-emphasis on controls

2 Avoid public criticisms of individuals

3 Ensure Herzberg's hygiene factors are catered for – the physical and psychological well-being of people should have high priority

4 Control systems should only be introduced where necessary

5 Give people an input into decisions which affect their working lives (especially in respect of substantial change)

6 Keep units and sub-units as small as possible (for large units tend to be bureaucratic and demotivational if they lack inspired leaders)

7 Pay attention to job design – avoid repetitive work, introduce variety

8 Give people autonomy and a job with a 'product' that an individual can recognise as his/her own

9 Ensure an individual understands the significance of their job in relation to the whole, which will also encourage new ideas and innovation.

Provide fair rewards

Although it is difficult to ensure that the financial reward an individual receives is fair (commensurate with contribution), effort must be applied in trying to get it right. There are other motivating 'returns' that individuals look for from jobs (as in Maslow's hierarchy of needs), but money is the one which has the main strategic importance for most people.

Most individuals like the combination of a fixed salary with a variable element related to performance or profits.

Also of tactical importance are incentives to improve performance in key areas eg sales, customer service and credit control.

Incentives can be in the form of cash, vouchers, merchandise or travel, but care must be taken to administer any incentive schemes fairly and without risking demotivating any 'losers'.

In providing fair rewards, an organisation should ask itself:

1 **Do we have a scheme whereby financial reward is made up of a fixed and variable element?**

2 **Do we link performance and pay?**

3 **Have we addressed the problems of whether to pay performance-related elements to the team or the individual?**

4 Do we actively consider changing our information systems to improve methods of rewarding performance?

5 Do we have schemes other than for sales people?

6 Does our organisation reward the behaviours/performance that publicly it values?

7 Do senior managers have pay rises/bonuses when they expect others to do without them?

It is always worth remembering Herzberg's insight that salary has more power to make people dissatisfied or unhappy than it has the power to motivate them.

Give recognition

Financial reward is seen by the recipient as a tangible form of recognition. There are other ways whereby appreciation is expressed for what has been contributed.

If recognition is not given, an individual can feel unnoticed, unvalued and unrewarded. This leads to a drop in motivation and energy levels.

Recognition should be formal or informal, for the individual and/or the team, as appropriate.

In giving recognition, you should try to ensure that you:

1 treat everyone in a fair and equal way

2 reward real achievements or contributions

3 reflect the core values of the organisation

4 use it to guide and encourage all concerned

5 give it in public if possible

6 give it formally and informally

7 give it genuinely and sincerely.

Other than financial payments, any words of recognition could be reinforced by giving:

- time off (with pay)
- tickets for an event or dinner out
- small gift
- special project of importance
- a change in job title.

It is a good idea to back up words of praise or recognition with some tangible gift.

Find out what is going on, share praise received with subordinates, and say thank-you more often, because people really value positive recognition and are motivated by it.

Know people's names – that is the basic form of recognition!

Summary and six-month follow-up test

To draw the best out of people you need to:

- be motivated yourself
- select people who are already motivated
- set challenging but realistic targets
- remember that progress motivates
- treat each person as an individual
- provide fair rewards
- give recognition.

Six-month follow-up test

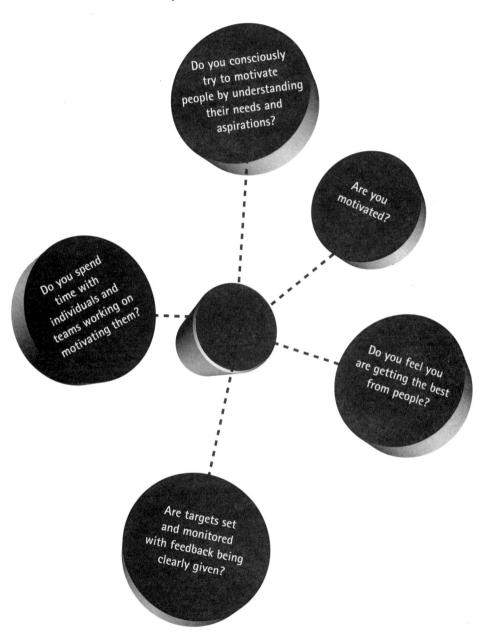

Do you consciously try to motivate people by understanding their needs and aspirations?

Are you motivated?

Do you spend time with individuals and teams working on motivating them?

Do you feel you are getting the best from people?

Are targets set and monitored with feedback being clearly given?

Chapter 8

Communication and presentation

Introduction

It is self evident that written and spoken communication skills are of crucial importance in business (and personal) life. Managers and leaders in particular must be effective communicators, good at getting their message across to, and at drawing the best out of, people. Communication skills in all forms, including non-verbal communication, need to be worked at and improved to ensure you understand people and they understand you.

Issues in communication

- You must be in social contact with the other person or people

- You must want to communicate

- It is better to risk familiarity than be condemned to remoteness

- The best way to empower others is to impart information (along with the delegated authority to make decisions and act on the information given)

- Get out of your office – meet, listen, provide information and give people the context in which they operate – to communicate and encourage

- Good communication is the core of customer care

- Remember customers (and suppliers) communicate with others about you

- To communicate with your customers you must handle complaints (as an organisation) as personally as possible – by a meeting or phone call in preference to letter or fax; you must listen to what customers suggest and communicate product/service changes/developments with them in advance

- Presentation skills are important in communicating with colleagues as well as customers/clients

- Meetings, internal and external are key indicators of a person's communication (including listening) skills

- Communication is a business requirement: establish proper systems and ensure all use them

- Remember the equation: size + geographical distance = communication problems

- Communicate with poor performers to improve their contribution and in appraisals be truthful, helpful and tactful

- Help others to improve their communication skills

- Assess your own communication skills and strive to improve them bit by bit. (Also, assess the communication skills of colleagues and identify areas for improvement).

Personal communication skills checklist
YES   NO

Do you understand the importance of communication in your personal and business life?

Are you a good communicator? (Check with your partner at home, with friends and with colleagues).

Can you write down your strengths and weaknesses as a communicator? And have you listed them?

Have you identified a need to improve your communication skills in any or all of these areas and will you now set about doing so (reading further books and/or attending training seminars as needs be):

- listening
- reading
- writing
- one-to-one interviews
- speaking and presentation
- managing meetings
- within your organisation?

Are you motivated strongly to become an excellent communicator?

Listening

Listening has been called the forgotten skill in communication. It is more than just hearing, it is the giving of thoughtful attention to another person whilst they are speaking.

The 'disease of not listening' – the 'I hear what you say' response – exhibits the following symptoms:

- Selective listening is habit forming: not wanting to know things and turning a deaf ear to certain types of information does two things:

  i) you do not listen to important items

  ii) people censor what they tell you

  and both can be damaging in business and in private life

- The constant interrupter is not listening (but planning his/her own next interruption)

- The 'day-dreamer' is not a listener

- The poor listener is easily distracted by external factors eg noise, heat/cold

- The lazy listener makes no effort with difficult information

- The poor listener over-reacts to a speaker's delivery and/or quality of visual aids rather than concentrating on what is being said.

The tell-tale signs of a good listener:

- paying close attention to others when they are talking
- taking an interest in someone you meet for the first time, trying to find an area of mutual interest
- believing everyone has something of value to teach or impart to you
- setting aside a person's personality/voice in order to concentrate on what they know
- being curious in people, ideas and things
- encouraging a speaker (with nods or eye contact)
- taking notes
- knowing one's own prejudices and working at controlling them to ensure listening continues
- being patient with poor communicators
- not being told you don't listen
- having an open mind in respect of other peoples' points of view

Listening skills centre on the five following attributes:

1 **Being willing to listen**

2 **Clearly hearing the message**

3 **Interpreting the meaning (the speaker's meaning, not only your interpretation)**

4 **Evaluating carefully (suspending judgement at first but then assessing value and usefulness)**

5 **Responding appropriately – remembering communication is a two-way street.**

In active listening you must be prepared to:

- ask questions

- weigh the evidence

- watch your assumptions

- listen between the lines (at what is not said *and* for non-verbal elements such as facial expressions, tone, posture, physical gestures etc.)

Reading skills

Good reading is listening in action – giving time and thought and remaining alert to the possibilities suggested. A good reader will try to work past:

- poor structure and layout

- boring style

- off-putting tone

- too much or too little information

- difficult to follow content

- inordinate length

- lack of illustrations/diagrams.

You should examine what materials you **must** read, **should** read or **might** read in the light of your job/role/future ambitions and then decide accordingly how and when to handle a particular item.

Speed reading is useful but only if it is accompanied by speed understanding and reading too fast (or too slowly) can impair understanding.

Read selectively (according to the must, should or might categorisation) from each item that confronts you. In this, scanning can help decide what attention to give particular items, so you should look at overall content (headings and sub-headings), sample the style and content of a few paragraphs, scan (if still interested) selected parts and then read that which you decide you are interested in. In reading carefully, you should be aware of the need to:

- be clear about your purpose of reading any piece of writing

- have questions in mind

- keep the questions firmly in mind and seek answers to them

- read for main ideas

- test the evidence, explanations and conclusions critically

- make notes as you progress

- test the writer's experience against your own

- consider whether or not to re-read

- discuss the material with others if appropriate

- reflect on what has been read.

Writing skills

Communicating in writing is an essential part of your job. There are three key elements in communicating on paper:

- Structure and lay-out

- Content

- Style and tone.

Writing should be thought of as talking to a person on paper and the six principles of good spoken communication apply – and they are:

1 **Clarity**

2 **Planning and preparation**

3 **Simplicity**

4 **Vividness**

5 Naturalness

6 Conciseness.

In letters, reports and memos the quality improves if the appropriate amount of planning is given to the points you wish to make and their order of importance. Further drafts can improve on the initial effort.

In writing a business letter you should always test the draft to ensure that:

1   the message is clear

2   points are made in the best order

3   it has the right style and tone

4   the most appropriate words and phrases are being used

5   the grammar/spelling is correct

6   the layout is attractive.

In writing reports which work the following points should be borne in mind:

- If the report is to stand alone and not to support a briefing or presentation it will need to be more than an aide-memoire

- A report should:

  - have an introduction with background and objectives

  - a title which indicates its purpose

  - be structured like a book with chapters, headings and sub-headings all clearly numbered and signposted

  - ensure the main body of evidence is succinct and arranged in an easy to follow order

  - end off with conclusions and recommendations

  - indicate assumptions made

  - put complicated data into an appendix

  - use illustrations/diagrams to clarify points made

- Easy reading makes hard writing
- Churchill's guidelines for report writing centred on:
  - setting out main points in a series of short, crisp paragraphs
  - complicated factors or statistics should form an appendix
  - considering submitting headings only, to be expanded orally
  - avoiding woolly phrases, opting for conversational phrases
  - setting out points concisely aids clearer thinking
- Reports can be tested for their effectiveness as follows:
  - is the structure and layout clear and easy to follow?
  - is the content complete and does it:
    - state the purpose?
    - say when, by whom, for whom and with what scope it was prepared?
    - identify and address the problem clearly
    - ensure detail does not cloud the main issue
    - give sources for facts
    - use consistent symbols and abbreviations
    - use accurate figures
    - make clear statements
    - have conclusions which flow logically from facts and their interpretation
    - ensure other possible solutions are only abandoned with stated reasons?
  - in general
    - is the report objective?
    - are criticisms of its recommendations pre-empted?
    - is it efficient and business-like?

- does it offend anyone?
- can it be understood by a non-technical person?
- is it positive and constructive?
- does it point up the decision to be made and by whom?

The style and tone of written communications is important to ensure the message is put over, and received, clearly. Some rules are:

- keep it simple

- strive for clarity above all things (even above brevity)

- be natural

- be concise

- let the tone reflect your true feelings but beware being terse, curt, sarcastic, peevish, angry, suspicious, insulting, accusing, patronising or presumptious

- be courteous (cordial and tactful).

Speaking and presentation skills

Effective speaking

There are certain principles to be followed to increase the power of communicating or expressing thoughts in spoken words.

Adair's six principles of effective speaking	1	Be clear
	2	Be prepared
	3	Be simple
	4	Be vivid
	5	Be natural
	6	Be concise

Preparation is helped by asking the Who? What? How? When? Where? Why? of the speaking occasion to focus on the audience, the place, the time, the reasons giving rise to the occasion, the information that needs to be covered and how best to put it across.

Presentation skills

There are six clusters which form the main elements of good, effective presentation skills.

1 Profile the occasion, audience and location

You should ask yourself these questions:

- The occasion
  - what kind is it?
  - what are the aims of it?
  - what time is allowed?
  - what else is happening?
- The audience
  - do they know anything about you?
  - do you know its size?

- what do they expect?
- why are they there?
- what is their knowledge level?
- do you know any personally/professionally?
- do you expect friendliness, indifference or hostility?
- will they be able to use what they hear?

- The location
  - do you know the room size, seating arrangements, layout/set-up and acoustics?
  - do you know the technical arrangements for use of microphones, audio-visuals, lighting and whether assistance is available (and have you notified in advance your requirements)?
  - do you know who will control room temperature, lighting and moving people in and out
  - have you seen it/should you see it?

2 Plan and write the presentation

Elements to address are:

- Deciding your objective which needs to be
  - clear
  - specific
  - measurable
  - achievable in the time available
  - realistic
  - challenging
  - worthwhile
  - participative

- Making a plan with a framework which has:
    - a beginning (including introductory remarks, statement of objectives and relevance and an outline of the presentation(s))
    - a middle (divided into up to six sections maximum, ensuring main points are illustrated and supported by examples or evidence, use summaries and consider time allocation carefully – and test it)
    - an end (summarise, linking conclusions with objectives and end on a high note)

3 Use visual aids

As up to 50 per cent of information is taken in through the eyes, careful consideration should be given to the *clear*, *simple* and *vivid* use of audio-visuals.

Useful tips are:

- Overhead/projector slides help make a point and keep eye contact with an audience (look at the people not the slides)
- Only present essential information in this way (keep content to about 25 words or equivalent if in figures)
- Have them prepared with appropriate professionalism
- Know the order
- Use pictures and colour if possible
- Do not leave a visual aid on for too long

Some difficulties with the different types of audio-visual equipment are:

- Overhead projection: ease of use and flexibility can be offset by poor quality images and problems in using well

- 35mm slide projection: professional in appearance, good for large audience and easy to use with a remote control can be offset by the need for dim lights (making note-taking difficult) and lack of flexibility in changing order of viewing

- Flipcharts: are easy to use and informal but difficult to use successfully with large groups and generally do not look professional and take up time to use

- Computers/tape decks/videos: can provide variety but difficult to set-up and synchronise, especially without technical support

4 Prepare your talk

In preparing your talk you need to decide whether you are to present with a full script, notes or from memory. This depends on the occasion and purpose of the presentation but whichever method is chosen, it is always acceptable to refer to your fuller notes if needs be during a presentation. Notes on cards or on slides/flipcharts can be used as memory joggers if you present without notes. If you are required to read a paper, at least be able to look up occasionally. Remember that failing to prepare is preparing to fail.

5 Rehearse with others

Rehearsal is important, but not so much that spontaneity is killed and naturalness suffers, to ensure the presentation (and any audio-visual aid) is actually going to work in practice.

You should always visit the location if at all possible and check that everything works – knowing the location is as important as rehearsing the presentation, indeed it is an essential part of the rehearsal.

6 Delivery on the day

Overall you should ensure that your presentation's:

- **beginning** – introduces yourself properly, captures the audience and gives the background, objectives and outline of your talk.

- **middle** – is kept moving along (indicating whether questions are to be asked as-you-go or at the end) with eye contact over the whole audience, at a reasonable pace, with a varying voice and obvious enjoyment on your part.

- **end** – is signalled clearly and then goes off with a memorised flourish.

- **questions** – are audible to all (or repeated if not), answered with conciseness, stimulated by yourself asking some questions, dealt with courteously and with the lights on.

- **conclusion** – is a strong summary of talk and questions/ discussions and closes with words of thanks.

If you find you are nervous (and this is normal) experiencing fear and its physical manifestations, remember to:

1 Breathe deeply

2 Manage your hands

3 Look at your audience

4 Move well

5 Talk slowly

6 Compose and relax yourself

7 Remember that the audience is invariably on your side

8 Project forward to the end of the presentation and picture the audience applauding at the end.

One-to-one interviews

Such meetings have the common characteristics that they are (usually) pre-arranged, require preparation and have a definite purpose.

Unless it happens to be a dismissal, one-to-one interviews require that:

- both parties know the purpose of the meeting (notified in advance)
- information to be exchanged should be considered in advance and answers at the meeting should be honest
- as interviewer you should keep control: stick to the point at the issue and the time allocated and give the other party adequate time to talk (prompting by questions if necessary).

The structure of the interview should be as follows:

- the opening – setting the scene, the purpose and a relaxed atmosphere
- the middle – stay with the purpose, listen, cover the agenda
- the close – summary, agree action, end naturally not abruptly on a positive note.

Sometimes it is useful to ask the right questions to obtain the required information/exchange. Questions to use are the open-ended, prompting, probing, or what-if questions, whilst the ones to avoid (unless being used for specific reasons) are the yes/no, closed, leading or loaded questions.

In performance appraisal interviews the aim should be to give constructive criticism in the following way:

1 **In private**

2 **Without preamble**

3 **Simply and accurately**

4   **Only of actions that can be changed**

5   **Without comparison with others**

6   **With no reference to other people's motives**

7   **Without apology if given in good faith.**

In receiving constructive criticism you should:

1   **remain quiet and listen**

2   **not find fault with the criticising person**

3   **not manipulate the appraiser by your response (eg despair)**

4   **not try to change the subject**

5   **not caricature the complaint**

6   **not ascribe an ulterior motive to the appraiser**

7   **give the impression you understand the point.**

In handling criticism you should accept it and not ignore, deny or deflect it.

Managing meetings

Meetings are much maligned, but are they usually approached and handled as they should be?

In general terms any meeting needs:

- planning
- informality
- participation
- purpose
- leadership

if it is to work, and that is so whether the meeting is in committee or conference format.

A meeting must have a purpose and this can be one (or all) of the following:

- to pool available information
- to make decisions
- to let off steam/tension
- to change attitudes
- to instruct/teach.

Meetings must be prepared for:

1 Know in advance what information, reports, agenda, lay-out, technical data or equipment is required

2 Be clear about the purpose

3 Inform other participants of the purpose and share, in advance, relevant information/documents

4 Have a timetable and agenda (and notify others in advance)

5 Identify main topics with each having an objective

6 Make necessary housekeeping arrangements.

Chairing a meeting means that you should guide and control it having defined the purpose of it, gatekeeping the discussions as appropriate (opening it to some, closing it when necessary), summarising, interpreting and concluding it with agreed decisions, on time.

The chairman's role in leading/refereeing effective meetings is to ensure that the following elements are handled correctly:

1 *Aim* – after starting on time, to outline purpose clearly

2 *Plan* – to prepare the agenda (and allocate time)

3 *Guide* – to ensure effective discussion

4 *Crystallize* – to establish conclusions

5 *Act* – to gain acceptance and commitment and then to end on time.

Meetings are groupings of people and can develop their own personality. It can help to understand the personality of a particular grouping by reference to group:

- conformity

- values

- attitude to change

- prejudice

- power.

So that the method of running the meeting and making it effective depends on understanding and overcoming problems posed by the group personality.

Within your organisation

Organisations have a degree of permanence, hierarchy and formal communication. Informal communication supplements the formal communication that is needed in organisations.

The **content** of communication in organisations should be (in relation to):

1   **The task:**
    - the purpose, aims and objectives
    - plans
    - progress and prospects

2   **The team:**
    - changes in structure and deployment
    - ways to improve team work
    - ethos and values

3   **The individual:**
    - pay and conditions
    - safety, health and welfare
    - education and training

The **direction** of flows of communication within an organisation must be downward, upward and sideways.

Decisions on what to communicate should bear in mind the must-know priorities and distinguish them from the should-know or could-know lower priorities. The best method for must-know items is face-to-face backed by the written word.

Two-way communication should be used and encouraged to:

• Communicate plans/changes/progress/prospects

• Give employees the opportunity to change/improve management decisions (before they are made)

• Use the experience and ideas of employees to the full

• Understand the other side's point of view.

Summary and six-month follow-up test

Summary

i) **Personal reminders**

Effective speaking – six key principles:

1 Be clear

2 Be prepared

3 Be simple

4 Be vivid

5 Be natural

6 Be concise

Practical presentation skills require you to:

• profile the occasion, audience and location

• plan and write the presentation

- use visual aids (if appropriate)
- prepare your talk
- rehearse (with others if necessary)
- deliver on the day.

Good communicators are skilled at listening by:

- being willing to listen
- hearing the message
- interpreting the meaning
- evaluating carefully
- responding appropriately.

Effective writing has three elements:

1 Structure

2 Layout

3 Style.

and also needs the six key principles of:

1 Clarity

2 Planning

3 Preparation

4 Simplicity

5 Vividness

6 Naturalness

7 Conciseness.

Six-month follow-up test

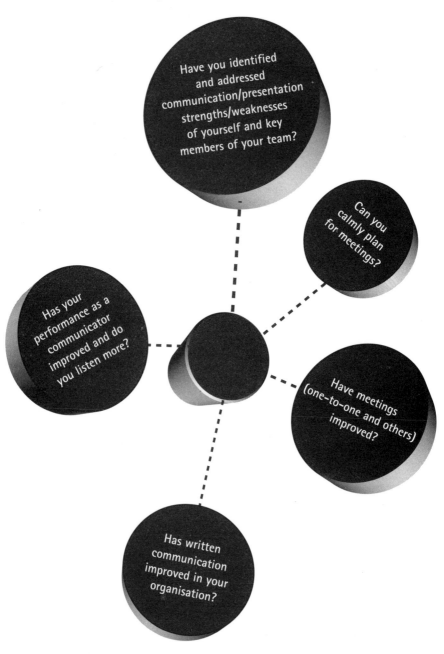

Have you identified and addressed communication/presentation strengths/weaknesses of yourself and key members of your team?

Can you calmly plan for meetings?

Has your performance as a communicator improved and do you listen more?

Have meetings (one-to-one and others) improved?

Has written communication improved in your organisation?

Chapter 9

Part 2: Personal reminders and thoughts worth thinking

Introduction

This section (as Chapter 5 in Part 1 did for the first part of the book) will look at the main areas covered in the second part of the book and will offer:

i) personal reminders – points to bear in mind in pursuing your personal development as a leader, motivator and communicator; and

ii) thoughts worth thinking – quotes from various sources which shed light on management and leadership topics covered in Part 2, which you might find helpful or inspiring.

Leadership and teambuilding

i) Personal reminders • Leadership

Whether in team, operational or organisational leadership, what matters is:

- The leader – qualities of personality and character
- The situation – partly constant, partly varying
- The team – the followers: their needs and values

Three overlapping and interacting circles of needs have to be focused on at all times:

Leadership functions (and the skills needed to exercise those skills) can be summarised as:

THE ROLE   FUNCTIONS

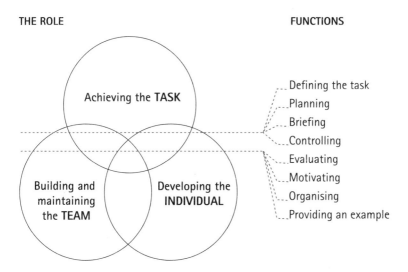

ii) Personal reminders · Teambuilding

Leaders should consider these issues in teambuilding:

Achieving the task

Achieving the task

- Purpose
- Responsibilities
- Objectives
- Programme
- Working conditions
- Resources
- Targets
- Authority
- Training
- Priorities
- Progress
- Supervision
- Setting an example.

Building and maintaining the team

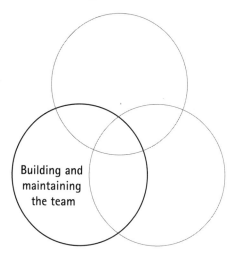

Building and
maintaining
the team

- Objectives
- Standards
- Safety standards
- Size of team
- Team members
- Team spirit
- Discipline
- Grievances
- Consultation
- Briefing
- Representing
- Supporting.

Developing the individual

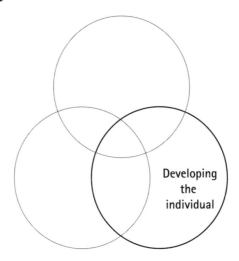

Developing
the
individual

- Targets
- Induction
- Achievement
- Responsibilities
- Authority
- Training
- Recognition
- Growth
- Performance
- Reward
- The task
- The person
- Time/attention
- Grievances
- Security
- Appraisal.

'Courage is the quality
that guarantees all others.'

Churchill

'Leadership is done
from in front.' Peter Young

'*As to moral courage, I have rarely met with the two-o'-clock-in-the-morning kind: I mean unprepared courage, that which is necessary on an unexpected occasion; and which, in spite of the most unforeseen events, leaves full freedom of judgement and decision.*'

Napoleon

'President Roosevelt possessed personality, but as his nation's leader... he also did his homework – thoroughly.'

'A sense of humility is a quality I have observed in every leader I have deeply admired.'

Dwight D Eisenhower

'What advice can be offered to a leader? He must discipline himself and lead a carefully regulated and ordered life. He must allow a certain amount of time for quiet thought and reflection; the best times are in the early morning, and in the evening. The quality, good or bad, of any action which is to be taken will vary directly with the time spent in thinking; against this, he must not be rigid; his decisions and plans must be adaptable to changing situations. A certain ruthlessness is essential, particularly with inefficiency and also with those who would waste his time. People will accept this, provided the leader is ruthless with himself...

Most leaders will find there is so much to do and so little time to do it; that was my experience in the military sphere. My answer to that is not to worry; what is needed is a quiet contemplation of all aspects of the problem, followed by a decision — and it is fatal to worry afterwards.'

Field Marshal Viscount Montgomery

'Is there not a difference between good leaders and leaders for good?'

John Lord

'A leader is best

When people barely know that he exists.

Not so good when people obey and acclaim him

Worst when they despise him

'Fail to honour people,

they fail to honour you,'

But of a good leader, who talks little,

When his work is done, his aim fulfilled,

They will all say, 'we did this ourselves.'

Loa Tzu • 6th century BC

'Quiet calm deliberation disentangles every knot.'

Harold MacMillan

'**Leaders should not**
be easily provoked.' St Paul

'The test of leadership is not to put
greatness into humanity but to elicit it, for
the greatness is there already.'

John Buchan

'He that gives good advice builds with one hand. He
that gives good counsel and example builds with both.
But he that gives good admonition and bad example,
builds with one hand and pulls down with the other.'

Francis Bacon

'It is almost true to say that leaders are 'made' – rather
than born.' Field Marshal Viscount Montgomery

'A good leader must be tough enough to win a fight, but not
tough enough to kick a man when he is down.'

W G Bennis and E H Schein

THE PRAYER OF A FAMOUS LEADER

'Lord, make me an instrument of your peace!

Where there is hatred, let me sow love,

Where there is injury, pardon;

Where there is doubt, faith;

Where there is despair, hope;

Where there is darkness, light;

Where there is sadness, joy.

O Divine Master, grant that I may not so much seek

to be consoled, as to console;

to be understood, as to understand;

to be loved, as to love.

For it is in giving that we receive;

It is in pardoning that we are pardoned;

It is in dying that we are born to eternal life.'   Francis of Assisi

'In managing human affairs, there is no better rule than self. restraint.'

Lao Tzu • 6th Century BC

If you can keep your head when those about you are losing theirs and blaming it on you.'

Kipling

'Your position never gives you the right to command. It only imposes on you the duty of so living your life that others can receive your orders without being humiliated.' Dag

Hammarskjold

ii) Thoughts worth thinking · Teambuilding

'You do not know me, I do not know you, but we have got to work
together. Therefore, we must understand each other, we must have confidence
in each other. I have only been here a few hours, but from what I have seen
and heard since I arrived, I am prepared to say here and now that I have
confidence in you. We will work together as a team. I believe that one of
the first duties is to create what I call atmosphere. I do not like the general
atmosphere I find here — it is an atmosphere of doubt, of looking back. All
that must cease. I want to impress upon everyone that the bad times are
over and it will be done. If anybody here thinks it cannot be done, let him
go at once. I do not want any doubters. It can be done and it will be done
beyond any possibility of doubt.'

Field Marshal Viscount Montgomery

*Extract from speech to staff in taking over the Eighth Army
before the Battle of El Alamein*

MORALE

Morale

　　Shows itself

　　As a state of mind

　　Radiating confidence

　　In people

Where each member

　　Feels sure of his own niche,

　　Stands on his own abilities

　　And works out his own solutions

　　– Knowing he is

　　Part of a team

Where no person

　　Feels anxiety or fear

　　Or pressure to be better

　　Than someone else

Where there exists

　　A sharing of ideas

　　A freedom to plan

　　A sureness of worth,

　　And a knowledge

　　That help is available

　　For the asking

To the end that

　　People grow and mature

　　Warmed by a friendly climate　　Anon

'**Light** is the **task,** when **many** share the **toil.**'

Homer

Motivation and people management

i) Personal reminders

To draw the best out of people the key strategies are:

- Be motivated yourself
- Select people who are already motivated
- Set challenging but realistic targets
- Remember that progress motivates
- Treat each person as an individual
- Provide fair rewards
- Give recognition

ii) Thoughts worth thinking

'The two great movers of the human mind are the desire of good and the fear of evil.'

Samuel Johnson

'I am persuaded that every being
has a part to play on earth:
to be exact, his or her own part
which resembles no other.' André Gide

'Such is the state of life that none are happy but by the anticipation of change.'

Samuel Johnson

'A man has one eye on what he gives, but seven eyes on what he receives.' Old German Proverb

'A man's reach should exceed his grasp.'

Robert Browning

'If you treat people as they are, they will stay as they are. But if you treat them as they ought to be, they will become bigger and better persons.'

Goethe

'Give me a **fire** and I will give you **light**'

Old Arab Proverb

'**Nothing great was ever achieved without enthusiasm.**'

Emerson

'*No man will find the best way to do a thing unless he loves to do that thing.*'

Old Japanese Proverb

'It is not enough to do our best. Sometimes we have to do what is required.'

Churchill

'Management, above everything else, is about people.

It is about the accomplishment of ends and aims by

the efforts of groups of people working together. The

people and their individual hopes and skills are the

greatest variable and the most important one.'

Sir John Harvey-Jones

'You get more of the behaviour you reward. You don't get

what you hope for, ask for, wish for, or

beg for. You get what you reward.'

Michel le Boeuf

'Fame is the spur that the clear spirit doth raise...

To scorn delights and live laborious days.' Milton

'Any of us will put out more and better ideas

if our efforts are fully appreciated.'

Alexander F Osborn

'No man does anything from a single motive.'

Samuel Taylor Coleridge

'BY ASKING THE

IMPOSSIBLE WE OBTAIN

THE BEST POSSIBLE.'

Italian proverb

'All

that we do

is done

with an eye

to something else.'

Aristotle

Communication and presentation

i) Personal reminders

Effective speaking – six key principles:

1 Be clear

2 Be prepared

3 Be simple

4 Be vivid

5 Be natural

6 Be concise

Practical presentation skills require you to:

- profile the occasion, audience and location
- plan and write the presentation
- use visual aids (if appropriate)
- prepare your talk
- rehearse (with others if necessary)
- deliver on the day

Good communicators are skilled at listening by:

- being willing to listen
- hearing the message
- interpreting the meaning
- evaluating carefully
- responding appropriately

Effective writing has three elements:

1 Structure

2 Layout

3 Style

and also needs the six key principles of:

1 Clarity

2 Planning

3 Preparation

4 Simplicity

5 Vividness

6 Naturalness

7 Conciseness.

ii) Thoughts worth thinking

'Speak properly, and in as few words as you can, but always plainly; for the end of speech is not ostentation, but to be understood.' William Penn

'Communication is the art of being

UNDERSTOOD.'

Peter Ustinov

'What is conceived well is expressed clearly

And words to say it will arise with ease.'

Nicholas Boileau

'If any man wishes to write in a clear style, let him first be clear in his thoughts.'

Goethe

'*Have something to say and say it as clearly as you can. That is the only secret of style.*'

Matthew Arnold

'Reading

is to the **mind**

what **exercise**

is to the **body.'**

English Proverb

'The major mistake in communication is to believe
that it happens.' George Bernard Shaw

'In good communication, people should be in no doubt

that you have reached a **conclusion.'**

John Adair and Neil Thomas

Thorogood publishing

Thorogood publishes a wide range of books, reports, special briefings, psychometric tests and videos. Listed below is a selection of key titles.

Desktop Guides

The marketing strategy desktop guide *Norton Paley* • £16.99

The sales manager's desktop guide
Mike Gale and Julian Clay • £16.99

The company director's desktop guide *David Martin* • £16.99

The credit controller's desktop guide *Roger Mason* • £16.99

The company secretary's desktop guide *Roger Mason* • £16.99

The finance and accountancy desktop guide *Ralph Tiffin* • £16.99

The commercial engineer's desktop guide *Tim Boyce* • £16.99

The training manager's desktop guide *Eddie Davies* • £16.99

The PR practitioner's desktop guide *Caroline Black* • £16.99

Win new business – the desktop guide *Susan Croft* • £16.99

Masters in Management

Mastering business planning and strategy *Paul Elkin* • £14.99

Mastering financial management *Stephen Brookson* • £14.99

Mastering leadership *Michael Williams* • £14.99

Mastering marketing *Ian Ruskin-Brown* • £16.99

Mastering negotiations *Eric Evans* • £14.99

Mastering people management *Mark Thomas* • £14.99

Mastering personal and interpersonal skills *Peter Haddon* • £14.99

Mastering project management *Cathy Lake* • £14.99

Business Action Pocketbooks

Edited by David Irwin

Building your business pocketbook	£6.99
Developing yourself and your staff pocketbook	£6.99
Finance and profitability pocketbook	£6.99
Managing and employing people pocketbook	£6.99
Sales and marketing pocketbook	£6.99
Managing projects and operations pocketbook	£6.99
Effective business communications pocketbook	£6.99
PR techniques that work	*Edited by Jim Dunn* • £6.99
Adair on leadership	*Edited by Neil Thomas* • £6.99

Other titles

The complete guide to international accounting standards
Ralph Tiffin and David Young • £18.99

The complete guide to debt recovery *Roger Mason* • £12.99

The John Adair handbook of management and leadership
Edited by Neil Thomas • £12.99

The inside track to successful management
Dr Gerald Kushel • £12.99

The pension trustee's handbook (3rd edition) *Robin Ellison* • £25

Boost your company's profits *Barrie Pearson* • £12.99

Negotiate to succeed *Julie Lewthwaite* • £12.99

The management tool kit *Sultan Kermally* • £10.99

Working smarter *Graham Roberts-Phelps* • £14.99

Test your management skills *Michael Williams* • £15.99

The art of headless chicken management
Elly Brewer and Mark Edwards • £6.99

Everything you need for an NVQ in management
Julie Lewthwaite • £22.99

Customer relationship management

Graham Roberts-Phelps • £14.99

Sales management and organisation *Peter Green* • £10.99

Telephone tactics *Graham Roberts-Phelps* • £10.99

Companies don't succeed people do!

Graham Roberts-Phelps • £12.99

Inspiring leadership *John Adair* • £15.99

The book of ME *Barrie Pearson and Neil Thomas* • £14.99

Dynamic practice development *Kim Tasso* • £19.99

Gurus on business strategy *Tony Grundy* • £14.99

The concise Adair on leadership *Edited by Neil Thomas* • £9.99

The concise time management and personal development

Adair and Melanie Allen • £9.99

Successful selling solutions *Julian Clay* • £12.99

Gurus on marketing *Sultan Kermally* • £14.99

The concise Adair on communication and presentation skills

Edited by Neil Thomas • £9.99

High performance consulting skills *Mark Thomas* • £15.99

Developing and managing talent Sultan Kermally • £14.99

Thorogood also has an extensive range of reports and special briefings which are written specifically for professionals wanting expert information.

For a full listing of all Thorogood publications, or to order any title, please call Thorogood Customer Services on 020 7749 4748 or fax on 020 7729 6110. Alternatively view our website at **www.thorogood.ws**.

BUSINESS SEMINARS

Focused on developing your potential

Falconbury, the sister company to Thorogood publishing, brings together the leading experts from all areas of management and strategic development to provide you with a comprehensive portfolio of action-centred training and learning.

We understand everything managers and leaders need to **be, know and do** to succeed in today's commercial environment. Each product addresses a different technical or personal development need that will encourage growth and increase your potential for success.

- Practical public training programmes

- Tailored in-company training

- Coaching

- Mentoring

- Topical business seminars

- Trainer bureau/bank

- Adair Leadership Foundation

The most valuable resource in any organisation is its people; it is essential that you invest in the development of your management and leadership skills to ensure your team fulfil their potential. Investment into both personal and professional development has been proven to provide an outstanding ROI through increased productivity in both you and your team. Ultimately leading to a dramatic impact on the bottom line.

With this in mind Falconbury have developed a comprehensive portfolio of training programmes to enable managers of all levels to develop their skills in leadership, communications, finance, people management, change management and all areas vital to achieving success in today's commercial environment.

What Falconbury can offer you?

- Practical applied methodology with a proven results
- Extensive bank of experienced trainers
- Limited attendees to ensure one-to-one guidance
- Up to the minute thinking on management and leadership techniques
- Interactive training
- Balanced mix of theoretical and practical learning
- Learner-centred training
- Excellent cost/quality ratio

Falconbury In-Company Training

Falconbury are aware that a public programme may not be the solution to leadership and management issues arising in your firm. Involving only attendees from your organisation and tailoring the programme to focus on the current challenges you face individually and as a business may be more appropriate. With this in mind we have brought together our most motivated and forward thinking trainers to deliver tailored in-company programmes developed specifically around the needs within your organisation.

All our trainers have a practical commercial background and highly refined people skills. During the course of the programme they act as facilitator, trainer and mentor, adapting their style to ensure that each individual benefits equally from their knowledge to develop new skills.

Falconbury works with each organisation to develop a programme of training that fits your needs.

Mentoring and coaching

Developing and achieving your personal objectives in the workplace is becoming increasingly difficult in today's constantly changing environment. Additionally, as a manager or leader, you are responsible for guiding colleagues towards the realisation of their goals. Sometimes it is easy to lose focus on your short and long-term aims.

Falconbury's one-to-one coaching draws out individual potential by raising self-awareness and understanding, facilitating the learning and performance development that creates excellent managers and leaders. It builds renewed self-confidence and a strong sense of 'can-do' competence, contributing significant benefit to the organisation. Enabling you to focus your energy on developing your potential and that of your colleagues.

Mentoring involves formulating winning strategies, setting goals, monitoring achievements and motivating the whole team whilst achieving a much improved work life balance.

Falconbury – Business Legal Seminars

Falconbury Business Legal Seminars specialises in the provision of high quality training for legal professionals from both in-house and private practice internationally.

The focus of these events is to provide comprehensive and practical training on current international legal thinking and practice in a clear and informative format.

Event subjects include, drafting commercial agreements, employment Law, Competition Law, intellectual property, managing and in-house legal department and international acquisitions.

For more information on all our services please contact Falconbury on +44 (0) 20 7729 6677 or visit the website at: www.falconbury.co.uk.

Adair t
Leadership Foundation

There is a revolution in progress as we move from management (old-style) to business leadership – using 'business' in the widest sense.

The Adair Leadership Foundation has been established to provide a centre of excellence for the philosophy and practical approach to leadership development that is associated with John Adair's name.

Its proven models and practical methods have stood the test of time and produced impressive results. At the Adair Leadership Foundation we believe that investment in leadership is the key to success in any organisation, while at the same time developing your key asset – people.

The Adair Leadership Philosophy

John Adair pioneered the 'Action-Centred Leadership' approach that has been applied successfully in organisations of all sizes at all levels.

Good leaders and managers should have full command of the three main areas of the Action-Centred Leadership model and be able to use each of the elements according to the right situation. Being able to do all of these things whilst keeping the right balance gets results, builds morale, improves quality and develops teams and productivity.

Although John Adair's leadership philosophy was conceived over 30 years ago, it has been continually improved to ensure it is still the best in the world. Its contribution to your organisation will ensure that you are competitive in today's challenging business environment.

The Adair Leadership Foundation Faculty

The faculty consists of specialists in the field of leadership who have shared John Adairs philosophy for many years. They have a great depth of understanding of how the philosophy can be successfully applied at different levels and in many types of organisation together with many practical examples and tips to help others benefit.

Accessing Adair Leadership Development

- **Practical and applied public training courses**
- **In-company tailored training programmes**
- **Coaching and mentoring**
- **Train the Trainer Programmes**
- **Consultation with John Adair**

For more information please call the Foundation on: 020 7729 6677 or visit the website at www.falconbury.co.uk